BIG
WITCH
ENERGY

✳

POWER SPELLS FOR
MODERN WITCHES

BIG
WITCH
ENERGY

✳

Semra Haksever

Illustrations by Olivia Healy

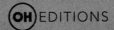

CONTENTS

HELLO AND WELCOME!

My intention with this book is to invite you to summon your 'Big Witch Energy' (BWE).

BWE calls for you to recognise the abundance of power that is within you, to practise radical self-acceptance, be comfortable and confident in your skin and to question society's expectations of you.

Many of the spells and rituals that you will find within this book are inspired by countless conversations over the years with friends, clients and customers. I see the same challenges and disempowering beliefs show up time and time again, ranging from feelings of low self-worth to struggling to create boundaries, shame around our bodies, a fear of ageing, pressure to follow society's expectations of us . . . I'll stop with the examples, but I am sure you can imagine how the list could go on.

The fact is, life isn't 'one size fits all'. We are all unique and our life paths are so different, yet the pressure to look a certain way and live our lives in a singular way is limiting and can leave us feeling as though we are failing.

My hope is that this book inspires you to tap into a little magic, helping you to challenge these thoughts, beliefs and societal expectations. Let's awaken our BWE and question patriarchal conditioning, fight oppression and the injustices in the world, and nourish ourselves while doing it.

The patriarchal system has never been a friend of witches – just think about that painful time in history when innocent people (mainly women) were accused of witchcraft. They were persecuted and murdered for not living within the patriarchal realms, daring to be unmarried, childless, sexually active or known for speaking up and using their voices.

It's impossible to not draw the conclusion that people in today's world who connect to the witch archetype have also felt persecuted or judged by our patriarchal system at some point in their lives. And that's why I chose to call this book *Big Witch Energy*. Rather than hiding our witch identities for fear of oppression, let's embrace the power it gives us, walk with the swagger of knowing we're well-endowed with magic. The patriarchy fears powerful women, women who've seen the fragility of their structures and are ready to tear them down. Witchcraft is the ultimate patriarchy survival tool, bringing a sense of healing, empowerment and connection to your life.

BWE is not 'woo woo' or any other cutesy description that minimises the power of this energy. Let's use it to acknowledge, honour and embrace the lineage and power that the symbol of the witch holds as we step in to our own BWE.

May the spells and rituals in this book create life-changing energetic shifts which will empower your own life and beyond.

I truly believe witches have the power to change the world.

Love, Semra x

HOW TO USE
THIS BOOK

How you approach this book is largely up to you. You can either follow these spells to the exact measurements, or you can be a maverick at the altar and adapt them however feels right for you.

I hope this is accessible to novice witches and offers something to the seasoned spellcaster too. Whichever you are, try not to worry about making mistakes; the most important thing is that you do everything with pure and good intentions. Here are some guidelines I try to keep in mind while practising magic. While not definitive, they're good to understand before beginning.

- Always allow magic to flow. Never force it.

- Respect magic. Only ever practise it when you can put your heart and soul into it, never because you feel you have to.

- If it's a New Moon and you want to set some intentions but you don't have the energy, wait until you feel like you are in the right mental place to do it, so you can focus and make it a memorable experience.

- Keep a Book of Shadows and record your spell-work so you can look back and repeat spells that have worked or tweak them as needed.

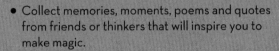

- Collect memories, moments, poems and quotes from friends or thinkers that will inspire you to make magic.

- Always acknowledge and respect different cultures and traditions; it is highly important to honour the roots of where your magic is inspired by.

- Share magic with the world. When you manifest, remember to not always make it all about you. Send wishes of good fortune and freedom to the whole world, acknowledging that we are all energetically connected.

- Remember: there is no such thing as sharing too much love and magic. Love and magic are both limitless. There is an endless supply of both.

- It is always important to remember that magic works in mysterious ways, and sometimes outcomes can show up in unexpected ways. Believe that the magic will work; never test it.

- And, most importantly, never forget that you are a cosmic force.

MAGIC ESSENTIALS

This section is all about what you'll really need to know when using this book, such as the herbs and flowers used, how to blend spells and how to use hot coal. Refer back here whenever you're unsure of something – and use the glossary on pages 152–154 for more information about each plant.

A Witch's Toolkit

There is no 'ideal' toolkit that I can describe here. You will find that your kit is forever growing. As you continue to create spells you might find you have a stronger connection to some herbs and aromas than others, and some might work for you and some might not; that is totally okay.

It's a good idea to store all your magical ingredients in one place. This could be wrapped up in a silk scarf, stored in a nice box or maybe you have a special cupboard or shelf designated to all of your magical ingredients, spell books and tarot cards.

Here is a list of the herbs, flowers, oils and tools needed for most of the spells in this book, which should be a good starting point if you're just creating your toolkit. Turn to page 152 for a more in-depth list of spell ingredients and all their magical correspondences.

Herbs, Flowers and Resins
Basil
Bay Leaves
Black pepper
Cardamom
Cayenne pepper
Chamomile
Cinnamon
Cloves
Frankincense
Ginger
Lavender
Mint
Mugwort
Myrrh
Nutmeg
Patchouli
Rose
Rosemary
Sage
Sandalwood
Thyme

Essential Oils
Bergamot
Chamomile
Jasmine
Patchouli
Rose
Sage

Tools
Pestle and mortar

Charcoal discs
Hot charcoal is used for burning herbal incense blends; there are quite a few of these spells in this book. Smoke represents the element of air in magic. It sends out powerful messages to the spirits and universe.

If you've never used it before, here's a quick overview. Hold the charcoal disc with some tongs (or tweezers) over a flame for 10–20 seconds or until it starts to spark, then place it in a heatproof vessel. Sprinkle a pinch of herbs and resins onto the disc.

If you don't have access to a heatproof vessel you can place a large cup of salt, sand or soil onto a ceramic or stoneware plate and place the hot coal on top of this.

Cauldron
To burn and blend spells in.

Tongs
Use these to heat up the coal (or you can use tweezers).

An assortment of coloured candles
If you don't have access to all the colours, just use white.

An assortment of coloured string
If you don't have access to all the colours, just use white.

Carrier oils
A carrier oil is often used in the mixing potions that will be anoint your body. You could use:
· Calendula
· Coconut
· Jojoba
· Sweet almond oil
· Thistle

Crystals
· Amethyst
· Black Tourmaline
· Clear quartz
· Lodestones
· Rose quartz

Black salt
To make black salt, blend hot charcoal remnants with regular salt.

RITUALS AND SPELL-WORK

When creating a ritual, you are sending a powerful and direct message of intent to the universe.

The aim of spell-work is to harness energy and shift your vibrational frequency so that it aligns with your intentions. Being completely focused and having total belief in what you are doing are the most potent components when creating a successful spell.

It is always important to remember that the level of energy you put into the spell is the energy that it will take on, so be confident when spell-casting and have a clear vision of your outcome. Try not to be nervous or scared as this can cause resistance, which will more than likely block the spell from working.

It is important to always respect magic. If you are creating a spell, give it time and space, don't rush it, and make it a special experience.

Set the scene ahead of a ritual and mark the time out in your calendar so that you won't be disturbed. Remember, gathering the components and setting the scene are part of the ritual. Candles, incense, your outfit and the soundtrack are all important components for a powerful ritual.

I recommend a little clean-up ahead of making magic, including an energetic cleanse with sage or rosemary and an actual clean-up of your physical space – there is nothing like post-ritual fresh sheets on the bed!

Also, notice if there is anything you wish to get rid of before the ritual. Remember that objects store energy, so sometimes having a clear-out of physical stuff can create space for whatever it is that you are calling in.

You may want to start with a bath, with a few drops of lemon, rosemary and sage essential oils added; this combination is always great for a body and energy cleanse.

Dress to impress. Wear something that feels empowering to you.

Next, set up an altar. Your altar can be created with images of any relating goddesses, gods or deities, crystals, salt, candles, incense or anything that feels special to you and will bring power to your magic. It could be one that is permanently set up or an altar that you are setting up especially for your ritual. If the latter is the case, you might want to set up the altar in the direction that corresponds with your spell or incorporates all the elements.

I will specify in each spell if there's a specific direction or element associated with it, but there's a broad guide here.

North Associated with earth. Personal growth, grounding, safety, home, prosperity and abundance are all linked to the north.

East Associated with air. East has links to healing, new beginnings, strength, clarity and rebirth.

South Associated with fire. Connected to passion, love, sex, strength, courage, protection and creativity.

West Associated with water. Healing, new beginnings, divination and spiritual guidance are linked to the west.

GROUNDING

Spell-work can make you a little giddy, so it is important to ground yourself, connect to the earth and everything that is beneath your feet, and feel centred in your body so that you can focus on the magic.

To do this, close your eyes and imagine that you are a giant tree standing in the centre of a field. Start by noticing what season it is, whether your branches have flowers or leaves. Imagine that your feet form the trunk, and coming out of them are your roots.

Feel your roots coming out the soles of your feet and travelling down, pushing through the ground and down into the earth. Imagine the roots passing soil, rocks, mantle, metals and through the Earth's crust, travelling all the way down . . . visualise them shooting down 6,378 kilometres, all the way down to the Earth's core. Reflect on that feeling of connection.

MANTRAS AND AFFIRMATIONS

Repeating mantras and affirmations can be another powerful way to centre yourself and get focused. For example, repeating 'I am love' for 5-10 minutes with your eyes closed is a simple but powerful statement.

Alternatively, you could use:
'I am grounded.'
'I am protected.'
'I am safe.'
'I am worthy of good things.'
'I am magical.'
'I am unstoppable.'
'It is okay for me to state my needs.'

... or whatever else relates to the magic you are going to make.

Acknowledging spirit guides and ancestors, known and unknown, can also help to raise the magical frequency. You might want to ring a bell or clap your hands to call in their presence, then ask them for guidance and protection to assist with your spell-work.

Frankincense is great for connecting to the spirits; burn some frankincense resin or anoint a purple candle with some frankincense essential oil as an offering to the spirits.

At the end of a ritual you can ring a bell or clap your hands and state out loud that 'the magic is done'. You may want to pat your body down and stamp your feet to bring yourself back into your body. (There's more on connecting to deities and spirits on pages 143-149).

VISUALISING

Visualising is a common technique in rituals and spell-work that requires you to close your eyes and tune in to a visual image playing out in your mind's eye.

Sometimes tuning in this way isn't so easy, so if you find this technique challenging try to visualise something that you have seen and experienced many times before. For example, imagine that you are eating an apple. Close your eyes and recall the memory of holding it in your hand, connect to its colour, weight and texture, then taking a bite. Try to remember its smell, its crunch, its taste. Then imagine eating the apple in a particular place, such as in your kitchen, on a beach or at work. As you do so, take some time to notice your surroundings and sounds. This visualisation can then be shifted to eating an apple in the place or energy that you are trying to step into.

If you're struggling to see a visual reference, try to tap into your senses and emotions. You might be able to recall a feeling or emotion, linked with a memory, when you felt the energy that you are trying to connect to.

If you find tuning in this way impossible (which some people do, and that's okay), use a pen and paper to write out in detail or draw a picture describing what you would like to visualise.

What Does it Mean to be a Witch?

There are many ways to be a witch. To me, being a witch is a lifestyle rather something that I 'do'. My religion is believing in magic, energies, frequencies and the unseen, and that contributes to the way I live my life.

Witches travel through this life being in constant awe of nature, its magic and its power again and again (and again!). We believe in the powerful medicine of herbs and honour their magical properties. Witches have a strong connection with animals, ancestors and spirit guides, aware that they watch over us. We are always communicating with the universe, always noticing signs, signals and planetary placements.

Witches have a strong personal growth game, healing themselves and their bloodlines, and always appreciate the wisdom that comes from the depths of life. And, most importantly, they know how much power the word 'witch' holds and respect its lineage, history and all the witches who came before us.

WHAT TYPE OF WITCH ARE YOU?

There are many different ways to identify as a witch, depending on your passions, interests and beliefs. You might feel a connection to a particular type of witchcraft, more than one or a little bit of all of them. Read the list below and see which speak to you.

City Witch

Not all witches have access to as much nature as we would like, even if you are lucky enough to have a garden, so instead City Witches focus on creatively using powerful magic within their homes. They might use toilets for banishing or the soil of their indoor plants to bury seeds and grow their intentions, or work with the moon via a window box or skylight.

Kitchen Witch

These witches create their magic in the kitchen. Cooking is a ritual for these witches, calling on the power of food to nourish, heal and create magic. Kitchen Witches use recipes to set intentions and send energy into their food.

Divination Witch

This is a witch who tunes in to their psychic energy. They might use scrying tarots, oracle cards, pendulums or palms.

Solitary Witch

A Solitary Witch enjoys their own company and prefers to perform rituals alone.

Hedge Witch

A Hedge Witch carries a strong connection to the spirit world and holds a deep knowledge of the medicinal magic of plants. These witches are experts at creating plant-based healing tinctures, remedies and potions.

Cosmic Witch

A Cosmic Witch follows astrology and performs spells and rituals around the Moons and planetary placements.

Elemental Witch

An Elemental Witch uses the power of earth, fire, water and air in their magical rituals.

Wiccan Witch

Wicca is a modern, nature-based paganism founded by Gerald Gardner in his 1954 book *Witchcraft Today*. Wiccans celebrate pagan holidays, the changing seasons and the Wheel of the Year.

Eclectic Witch

If you have connected with more than one type of witch on this list, you are probably an Eclectic Witch. Eclectic Witches can pick and choose, taking wisdom from all forms of witchcraft and creating their own traditions.

A (VERY) BRIEF HISTORY
OF THE WITCH HUNTS

Between the fourteenth century and eighteenth century a complete miscarriage of justice happened throughout Europe (and later spread to America). Thousands of people – mainly women – were accused of witchcraft. These innocent people were hunted down and brutally tortured until they were forced to offer a false confession. Once they had confessed, they would be executed.

Up until this time, witches, sorcerers or 'cunning folk', as they were known, were respected pillars of the community. They were trusted wisdom-keepers, midwives, herbalists and healers, holding a deep knowledge of herbal folk magic, creating tinctures and potions to heal the sick. They suddenly found themselves being accused of witchcraft and worshipping the Devil.

Life for many became a paranoid free-for-all, and it wasn't just the practising witches who were being accused. People started blaming all their misfortunes on witches' curses; they became an easy scapegoat. The accused were often older, single, childless women. Suspicions would arise for the smallest reason: because a funny look had been given, a disagreement had taken place, because it had been observed that they weren't going to church, or perhaps they were going to church too often. Sometimes it was because the accused was too loud or too quiet, or they were simply in the wrong place at the wrong time. The paranoia and finger-pointing was endless.

Witches were blamed for just about anything, from extreme weather conditions to their neighbours not conceiving or their livestock dying.

The mass hysteria started to spread after the release of a handbook, *The Malleus Maleficarum* (*The Hammer of Witches*), by a German Catholic clergyman, Heinrich Kramer, in 1446. The handbook provided a guide for hunting and persecuting witches, stating that witches worshipped the Devil and were a huge threat to society. It claimed that women were morally weaker than men, which made them easier prey for the Devil.

The book was filled with overly sexualised and fantastical case studies. One of them recounted that a witch had been found to be cutting off and collecting penises and storing them in a bird's nest. When they were found in the nest, they were wriggling about! To think that this handbook, and this case study, was used as a factual reference in courts to convict and then execute those who were on trial is both heartbreaking and horrifying.

The accused stood no chance. And once someone had been accused, they would rarely be spared. They were stripped, scalped and searched for moles, birthmarks, scars or any other markings to trace a connection to the Devil. They were deprived of sleep for days while being continuously physically tortured. They were thrown in the river with their hands and feet tied together. If they floated, they were a witch, and if they drowned, they were innocent . . . but also dead.

A lot of money was made off the back of the trials by the courts, the executioners and self-titled 'witch hunters'.

Shockingly, there were an estimated 40,000–50,000 executions for witchcraft across Europe.

When I think about all of the innocent people who lost their lives in this deeply cruel and unfair way, I wonder what the accused would make of modern-day witches. We have to hope their spirits are watching over us, celebrating our freedom and supporting us reclaiming what it means to be a witch.

Big Witch Energy

Big Witch Energy (BWE) calls for you to be a witch who stands in their power and thrives. Call on your BWE to empower yourself and invoke the highest self-value. Step into that power and use magic to make the world a better place, celebrate the freedom that you have, raise consciousness, fight oppression and allow yourself to feel rage against the patriarchy.

These spells will help you connect with the best version of yourself and truly feel your power.

A SPELL TO SUMMON YOUR VOICE

You will need:
2 cups bath salts
  (Epsom, Himalayan
  or Dead Sea salt – or
  a mix of all)
9 drops of frankincense
  essential oil
your saliva
2 tbsp carrier oil
a red candle
something sharp, like a
  big pin/letter opener/
  athame/knife
salt
1 bay leaf
a mirror

The magic you create is divine; connect to it and pledge to always stay true to your BWE. For extra potency I would recommend spending some time meditating on what dedications of your own you would like to add.

This spell is best performed on a New Moon.

_____

Start this ritual with a cleansing bath. Add the bath salts to the water.

Create a playlist for your bath, with music that inspires you to go deep and that empowers you. I can recommend that some baroque music, such as Bach, will usually do the job!

Ask the bath to clear you of any energy that isn't serving you. If there is anything that is making you feel less powerful or is draining your energy, this is the time to let it go.

When you are ready to get out of the bath, pull the plug while you are still in it, watch the water disappear and feel it taking whatever it has cleansed down the plug hole with it.

Blend the frankincense, some saliva (about ½ a teaspoon) and the carrier oil. Heat the side of the candle and carve out a word, acronym or symbol to represent personal power (you could write your name with the word 'power' above and below it). Anoint the candle with the blended potion and surround its base with a circle of salt.

Light the candle and burn the bay leaf, blessing the candle with the bay leaf's smoke.

Stare at yourself in the mirror in the candlelight and say your name three times, then anoint the following areas:

Firstly, anoint your third eye with the blended potion and say, 'I will always see beyond what is in front of me.'

Then anoint your lips and say, 'I will always speak my truth.'

Next, anoint your heart and say, 'I will always practise love for myself so that I can love others.'

Then anoint both of your palms and say, 'I will always help and heal others when possible.'

Look at your palms, notice all the lines, and say, 'I appreciate my uniqueness.'

Then anoint your womb or stomach area to honour and send love to your grandmothers and your bloodline.

Then rub the potion on the soles of your feet and say, 'I promise to always walk in my own direction and trust my own unique path in life.'

If you have a goddess, god or deity who you wish to walk alongside you right now (see page 143-149), use this moment to ask them to walk alongside you, protect you and send you messages of encouragement.

EYE POWER

You will need:
3 chamomile tea bags
a bowl of hot water
a flannel or large
  muslin cloth

Use this spell to refresh your eyes and take back your power, to see situations in a new way.

———————

Steep the tea bags in the hot water for 5 minutes, then place the bowl in the fridge for 5-10 minutes.

When the chamomile water is chilled, soak a flannel or cloth in it. Squeeze out any excess water and fold the cloth in half. Lie down and place it over your eyes. For added magic, open your windows to hear nature, or if you are a 'city witch' play some bird sounds or nature sounds.

Open a dialogue with your higher self; remember your higher self won't judge and will only respond with complete compassion for yourself and others. Ask it to guide you through possible outcomes and know that the advice will always be caring, creative and full of love. Trust that your higher self will always show you a win-win outcome.

Allow the conversation to continue. When you have come to a solution, visualise it three times. Remove the cloth and see the world with fresh eyes.

A SPELL TO SUMMON YOUR VOICE

You will need:
a lapis lazuli crystal
a clear jar
9 cloves
15 drops of bergamot
  essential oil
50ml (1¾ fl oz) carrier oil
  of your choice

With this spell, call in the power to invoke your voice.

_____

Begin by adding the crystal and oils to the jar. As you add each clove, bless it by saying the following affirmation out loud:

'My voice matters.
I speak with integrity, and that is all that matters.
I speak the truth.
I am authentic.
I express myself clearly.
I speak with confidence.
I have the courage to express myself.
I talk without fear.
I communicate clearly.'

Charge this spell jar up under the sun or place it on an altar facing east for sunrise.

Having done this, rub the oil onto your throat and tune in to what it is that you wish to say. Know that you don't always have to please people, and that your feelings are completely valid. As you anoint this courage potion to your throat, repeat the affirmations.

A SPELL TO CLEAR PATRIARCHAL OBSTACLES

You will need:
pencil
paper
scissors
1 lemon, halved
9 tbsp vinegar
sharp knife
salt
pins or nails (optional)
a blue candle
9 drops of lavender
  essential oil

Patriarchy is the age-old system that sees men dominate and have power over women in all aspects of society. It is highly unfair and can cause major obstacles for, and exploit, women, gender non-conforming and other non-binary people. It is a system that is so ingrained in our society that it is often just accepted and not noticed.

Whether you are sacrificing your career to have a baby, recognising that an iPhone is designed for a man's hand, frustrated at the gender pay gap, annoyed at medicine's skew towards men's health or feeling like you are failing at life because you don't want to create a nuclear family... the list of how the patriarchy can diminish our self-worth goes on.

This spell helps you recognise and blast away the patriarchal structures in your way.

———————

Start this spell by writing out what you are angry about. Allow the frustration and rage to travel through your hands and onto the paper. When you have written it out, cut up the paper into tiny pieces.

Place the pieces of paper in a bowl and squeeze the lemon juice on them, then add the vinegar. (Don't throw away the lemon halves!) Stir in an anti-clockwise direction with a sharp knife. As you stir, allow yourself to feel a sense of relief as you visualise some of these systems dissolving.

When it feels right, scoop the paper out and place the pieces inside one of the empty lemon halves. Top the lemon up with salt, then affix the two lemon halves together, fastening it with pins or nails or just pressing the two pieces together. You can then dispose of this in a bin (not a bin inside your house).

Hopefully at this stage of the ritual your anger and rage will have been expelled, but if you are still feeling it, by all means go and scream into a pillow or throw several punches at a cushion.

Now for the second part. On the blue candle carve a message horizontally to anyone, or a situation, that is a victim of the patriarchy to whom you wish to send love, healing energy and empowerment, with an infinity symbol on each end.

Facing east, anoint the blue candle with lavender essential oil. Light the candle and place your hands on your heart. Stare into the flame and send out love, healing energy and cosmic vibes.

As the flame flickers and the candle burns, feel your abundant energy flowing from your open heart to where it is needed in the world.

A SPELL TO STOP
PEOPLE PLEASING

You will need:
a few pinches of
   rosemary
a few pinches of thyme
a pinch of orris root
1 charcoal disk

This is a spell to remind you that it is okay to put yourself before others.

Creating healthy boundaries and learning to say 'no' is a powerful way to allow the universe to see that you have a high level of self-worth. Remember, if you don't like the way something is playing out, if something has upset you or has made you feel disrespected, it is okay to say so!

As children we are taught to 'be good' and to not cause any trouble, which essentially means to be quiet and agreeable. But as witches we need to take up space, stand up for ourselves and make our voices heard.

Blend the ingredients and create an altar facing east.

Spend some time recalling times you have people-pleased and regretted it; you might think of times you have written 'I'm fine with whatever you want' in a message and not really meant it; you may think of times you wish you had spoken up but were scared you might upset someone or scare them off, or a time when you didn't respect yourself and create a clear boundary.

Sprinkle a pinch of the blend on some hot coal (see page 11). As it starts to burn, allow yourself to recall one of these memories. Create an image of it in your mind and see it playing out on a loop as if on a TV screen.

Take some deep breaths, inhale the aroma of the spell and ask to be sent a colour that embodies the energy of personal power.

When you have your colour in mind, visualise it filling up the TV screen and completely colouring over the memory that is playing out. Then, visualise this colour surrounding you. See it wrapped around you like a cloak and feel its empowering energy. As the smoke travels east, the direction of air, repeat the following to the smoke:

'It is okay to state my desires.
It is okay to state my desires.
It is okay to state my desires.'

Next time you find yourself in a situation where you feel like you need the cloak, all you have to do is close your eyes, visualise yourself putting it on and remember: it is okay for you to state your desires.

A SPELL FOR THE COLLECTIVE TO BANISH EXPLOITATION

You will need:
newspaper articles (or articles printed from the internet) with stories of exploitation
scissors
black paper/black envelope
skin from 1 bulb of garlic
1 tsp black pepper
1 tsp cayenne pepper
black string
angry energy flowing through your veins
12 drops sage essential oil (optional)

This one is for when you are feeling especially angry or triggered by injustice or exploitation in the world.

———

Take the article or print-out of the injustice that you wish to banish. Cut it up into tiny pieces and place in the centre of the black paper (or into the envelope), then add the garlic skin and cayenne pepper.

Fold the paper tightly, or seal the envelope, then wrap the string tightly around the paper. Tie three knots, and with each knot repeat what it is you wish to banish, then burn it and dispose of the ashes where nothing grows.

After a banishing spell like this, cleanse with rosemary or sage or take a cleaning bath with some salt and 12 drops of sage essential oil.

A SPELL TO
BANISH TYRANTS

You will need:
a photo of the tyrant
  or a piece of paper
a red pen
a bowl
8 peppercorns
a hammer or a rolling pin

How is it that corrupt tyrants seem to be running the world? Harness your energy of frustration, anger and injustice and use it in this spell.

––––––––––

Take the picture of the tyrant, or write their name out three times, and with the red pen draw a big cross over either their picture or their name.

Fill the bowl with water, add the peppercorns and put it in the freezer. When it has frozen, take it out of the freezer and shatter the ice with the hammer.

Rip up the picture or paper with angry hands. Place the pieces in some of the melted water and put it back in the freezer. Leave it in there for three moon cycles. Dispose of the remaining ice somewhere where nothing grows.

A SPELL TO TAKE UP SPACE

You will need:
9 cloves
9 drops of orange
  essential oil
1 tsp frankincense resin
1 charcoal disc

Use this spell to call on unapologetic energy; this is the antidote to being small. Use this spell to stand in your power and own it.

––––––––––

Blend the cloves, oil and resin in a clockwise direction then burn over hot coal (see page 11). Stand in front of a mirror in a superwoman-style stance: legs apart and hands on hips. Allow the smoke to travel around your body and surround your aura. Inhale the aroma, taking in its power and finding the courage to take up space.

As the smoke continues to travel, think of a time in your life that required courage. Focus on this feeling and connect to it, allowing the energy of the memory to radiate around your body. Make yourself a promise to do something out of the ordinary, something that is a challenge or something that inspires you.

A SPELL TO BANISH THE NEED FOR EXTERNAL VALIDATION

You will need:
5 drops of lavender
  essential oil
10 drops of orange
  essential oil
5 drops of chamomile
  essential oil
100 ml (3½fl oz) carrier
  oil of your choice
1 bay leaf

Use this spell to tune in to the energy that you are enough. You are a human and that's all you have to be. Invoke the power of not caring what anyone else thinks or says about it. You do you.

Blend the oils, then light the bay leaf over the potion and bless the potion with the smoke. Say out loud, 'I am human and I am enough,' taking the time to recognise that you don't have to be anything more than this.

Massage your body with the oils while repeating the mantra: 'I am human and I am enough.'

A SPELL
TO SUMMON
BOUNDARIES

You will need:
a black tourmaline crystal
thyme (a sprig or dried)
a pouch or scarf

Boundaries keep us safe and are important in spell-work and beyond. Spiritual people – including witches, healers and empaths – can sometimes have a challenging time setting boundaries, and the open-heartedness that magical beings possess can be taken advantage of.

Remember, it is okay to say 'no' without feeling guilty. You have the right to state your needs and deserve respect. Use this potion to help set boundaries, whether they are physical, spiritual, financial or to protect your precious time.

———————

Hold the black tourmaline and focus on the boundary you wish to set. Remember that it is okay to set boundaries and that you don't have to explain yourself. Focus on how setting this boundary will create space for energy that will help you thrive and for your intentions to grow.

Continue to hold the tourmaline and ask it to assist you with protecting your valuable energy. Place the thyme in the pouch or wrap it in a small scarf or piece of fabric, then ask it to give you the courage to speak up for yourself.

Place the crystal in the pouch with the thyme and carry it with you when you need its assistance.

A SPELL TO FIGHT THE INJUSTICE OF OPPRESSION

You will need:
9 crushed black
  peppercorns
10 drops of rosemary
  essential oil
3 pinches of dried sage
30ml (1fl oz) carrier oil
  of your choice
black candle
pen and paper

Blend the ingredients and anoint the candle with the blend. To do this, tip the blend onto a plate and roll the candle away from you in the blend.

Write on a piece of paper what it is you wish to banish, then burn the paper over the candle's flame. Dispose of the ash and candle remnants somewhere where nothing grows, or throw it in the bin.

MY BODY, MY CHOICE

An important part of flexing your BWE is getting political – fighting for equality, fighting for your human rights. All women face many political and societal pressures, such as abortion laws (and having reproductive rights taken away) or having to dress or behave in a certain way, and many other situations where you don't feel like you have agency over your body.

This is a spell for anyone who has felt powerless or betrayed by the system – use this spell to call your power back or send it out to whoever in the world might need it.

You will need:
a blue candle
pen and paper
a Justice tarot card for your altar

————

Light the candle and spend some time gazing at the flame, thinking about what needs justice and sending magical power to it. Write down what the perfect outcome would be on a piece of paper, then burn it with the candle's flame. Collect the ashes and sprinkle them on the Justice card.

Blow the candle out and repeat the previous steps over the next three nights. On the third night, collect the ash and sprinkle it while facing east, asking the element of air to bring change.

A QUICK REST
AND RESET

You will need:
an eye mask or a dark
  room
a quiet and technology-
  free space
a clear quartz crystal

Sometimes, resting is where the most powerful magic happens – giving yourself space to think, to just be. Nothing to do, just relax and rejuvenate and free yourself from the grind. Even 10 minutes a day can have a positive impact, and this will help you maximise that precious time.

Set an alarm for 10 minutes. Sit upright, with your back supported, in a dark room or with an eye mask on in a quiet space, free from the distractions of technology. Place one hand on top of the other facing upwards and cradling the crystal.

Close your eyes and just be still for a moment; if your mind is busy, just allow it to be. Allow whatever thoughts come to be there and just follow whatever direction they go.

PROTESTING
IS POWER

You will need:
9 drops of rosemary
   essential oil
9 drops of lavender
   essential oil
4 drops of mint
   essential oil
80ml (3fl oz) carrier oil
a glass bottle or jar

Showing up and going on a march or a rally is important. Connecting with people who share the same beliefs and want the same outcome as you do creates an empowering connective energy. Protesting can inspire a debate; it can bring about change and have a powerful impact. I always feel emotional at protests as I am reminded how much people care.

Use this potion to anoint yourself with power and protection on protests, marches and rallies.

Blend the oil in a clockwise direction. As you do this, allow the energy of the passion and belief for what you are protesting about to charm the potion.

Anoint yourself with this empowering oil as you protest, knowing that your voice in the crowd will make a difference.

A SPELL FOR WHEN YOU ARE GHOSTED

You will need:
jasmine essential oil

In the world of dating, being ghosted can be incredibly disempowering. This confusing energy and need for closure or answers can drain you and rob you of your BWE. Use this spell to take back your power and create your own closure, to assist with moving on and gaining a new perspective on your situation.

Think about your precious energy and how much time you are willing to give to someone who hasn't respected you. Know that when something like this happens, it is usually the universe protecting you.

Rub some jasmine essential oil on your third eye for clarity. Meditate on how you are worth more than this kind of treatment.

Visualise the 'ghost' in front of you and see yourself saying goodbye to them. If there is anything you want to say to them, do it now. If you had an energetic connection, you will probably feel a strong resistance in the pit of your stomach, but remind yourself that you are worth more. Watch them begin to fade away, visualise their body slowly vanishing.

Say out loud:
'I am worthy of more than this.
I am worthy of more than this.
I am worthy of more than this.'

Trust that the universe is looking out for you; trust that this is a big sign that your spirit guides are protecting you. Repeat this spell for three days.

Radical
Self–Love

Practising radical self-love is the ultimate power move when summoning your BWE.

To harness this superpower, you must allow yourself to step in to a frequency of compassion and connection to yourself. This is a place within yourself where no improvements or tweaks need to be made, but you experience complete contentment for all that you are at this moment in time.

I say 'practicising' because, for many of us, living in this energy isn't our go-to; it often takes a conscious awareness to celebrate ourselves rather than tear ourselves down. BWE energy calls for you to question why you haven't been taught to live in this energy.

Our personal persecutions come in many forms: negative self-talk, shame, not feeling comfortable in our skin or not fitting into a mould that society expects of us.

Just as witches were victims of persecution and hunted down in the Middle Ages - seen as outcasts, independent and not following societial norms - we too are victims of persecution when we don't fit the patriarchal mould.

Calling in our BWE and living our lives with this power is a tribute to those who lost their lives in the witch trials. The least we can do to honour them is to embrace ourselves and acknowledge our freedom, living our lives in the most wholehearted and authentic way we can, cultivating radical self-love inside and out.

RADICAL LOVE
FOR OUR BODIES

Conjuring body positivity with BWE calls for you to not only celebrate your body but to go a little deeper and question any resistance you may have to being comfortable in your skin and fully accepting of yourself.

Exploring this resistance and gaining awareness through the following rituals will hopefully bring a little clarity and empowerment to help you accept that your body is perfect just as it is.

Who set the beauty standards?
Who decided that the majority of people we see on television, in films and on social media should be slim, with flawless airbrushed skin and surgical enhancements?

Why is our view so limited?
Being bombarded with images that do not reflect the majority of us creates a restrictive vision of what is deemed to be 'attractive', and not living up to these standards can bring feelings of inadequacy.

It is time to question who made these rules.

These spells will help you rightly worship your body, giving it some much-deserved love and empowering you at the same time.

Let's start with a ritual to cleanse you of patriarchal ideas of what your body is supposed to look like.

METAMORPHOSE SCRUB

Use this to scrub away the old belief systems
that you have about your body. This unwelcome
energy no longer needs to squat in your energy
field. Let's shed it, create room and invite in
radical self-acceptance.

Before you begin, observe how you view your
body. Do your views come from outside sources,
such as comments from friends and lovers that
you have received over the years, are they based
on comparison with others, or are they your own
original thoughts?

Wherever these views came from, we need to
challenge any negativity or judgement within them.

You will need:

1 cup salt (sea salt, Epsom salts, table salt, Himalayan or a mix of all four is fine – just avoid the big granules)

1 cup oil (any oil is fine, but coconut, shea or almond is best)

5 drops of lavender essential oil

5 drops of rosemary essential oil

5 drops of lemon essential oil

Mix the ingredients together and use to exfoliate while in the bath or shower. Gently scrub away the patriarchal conditioning that has programmed you into thinking any part of your body isn't good enough, face any negative opinions you have had about yourself and banish any memories of damaging comments anyone has ever said to you about that beautiful body of yours.

As you wash away these feelings, notice how lovely and conditioned your skin feels as the rich oils soak in.

Embrace all the love you have for your magical skin vessel.

EMPOWERING FACE OIL

You will need:

30ml (1fl oz) argan oil
(jojoba or apricot kernel
would work well too)
8 drops of rose
essential oil
3 drops of chamomile
essential oil
3 drops of lavender
essential oil

This is a spell to honour all aspects of your perfectly imperfect face.

Blend all the oils in a glass jar or bottle, then stir in a clockwise direction.

Take some time to look in the mirror and study the lines, scars, freckles, bumps and the (im)perfections on your face. As you examine yourself, connect any scars, lines or marks to memories. Maybe some of the lines are from happy times, when you laughed so hard your belly ached, or maybe they are from a challenging time that taught you great lessons and deep wisdom. Try to see the history and positivity behind each feature of your face.

Massage your face with the potion, and as you do, chant three times:

'I bless the wonder of my face,
A true original.
Every feature is completely unique.
I bless the wonder of this skin,
And the wonder that lies within.'

PROTECTIVE SHIELD MOISTURISER

You will need:
400g (14oz) mango
   butter, coconut butter
   or almond butter
450ml (16fl oz) apricot oil
1 tsp vitamin E oil
10 drops of ginger
   essential oil
10 drops of black pepper
   essential oil
10 drops of clove
   essential oil

Use this body butter to activate a protective shield to help nourish your skin, keep you protected and repel negative energy. This takes a while to make, but it is a tried-and-tested recipe and I can guarantee that it will make your skin feel amazing!

Melt the mango butter and apricot oil in a bain-marie (or double boiler). When the butter and oils have melted, stir and put them in the fridge for 2 hours.

Remove and whip with a food processor for 20 minutes. Add the vitamin E oil and essential oils and blend for another 20 minutes. As you watch it whipping up, visualise white protective light beaming into the mixture.

When you apply it to your body, feel this light soaking in and filling you with protective energy.

Tip: If you don't want to make the body butter, you can just add the essential oils to some unscented moisturiser. Use half the amount of essential oils and add them to 1 cup of moisturiser.

'I AM' POTION

The number one most radical aspect of self-love is complete self-acceptance. No improvements to be made, no destination to get to, every bit of you is welcome as you are and you exist no matter what. You don't have to be better or to reach a specific goal. You just have to stand in your 'I Am' energy.

In this state you can accept that perfection doesn't exist, that it's okay to make mistakes. You can be lovely and you can also be crappy. You can be on top of the world and you can be sad. You can be motivated and you can be lazy. You can be messy, bored, inspired or anything else!

When you stand in your 'I Am' energy, you are in your own power. When you enter this empowering, energetic frequency, nothing but your pure existence matters.

To help you get closer to this stage, mix this potion in a glass jar or bottle.

You will need:

100ml (3½fl oz) carrier oil
  of your choice
15 drops of rose
  essential oil
10 drops of patchouli
  essential oil
a mirror

Mix the ingredients together. Holding the vessel in both hands, look in the mirror and say the following quotation out loud to the potion:

'You are loved just for being who you are, it's not something that needs to be earned. Your imperfections, errors or shortcomings do not matter. That love cannot be taken away from you. It will exist for ever.'

Then anoint yourself with the potion, repeating the words 'I am. I am. I am.'

Use this potion whenever you need it (or make a point of always performing this ritual on a Full Moon).

IMPOSTER SYNDROME BANISHING OIL

Imposter syndrome is no friend of BWE. It can bring up feelings of inadequacy, like you don't belong, or even make you feel as if you are a fraud and have fooled everyone into thinking that you are worthy to be where you are.

Let's banish that feeling and remind yourself that you are deserving and exactly where you are meant to be.

You will need:

pen and paper

a glass vessel

9 drops of cypress
essential oil

1 sprig of fresh thyme
(or a pinch of dried if
you can't get fresh)

9 drops of bergamot
essential oil

50ml (1¾fl oz) carrier
oil

Spend a bit of time writing out some of your life achievements or moments where you have felt proud of yourself; you should aim for at least five. These could also be previous times you have overcome imposter syndrome.

When your list is complete, blend the oils together in a clockwise direction. Hold the vessel containing the potion and say your name out loud three times, then read aloud everything you have written down.

Feel yourself shift into the vibrational frequency of being worthy. Continue to feel this energy and allow it to flow through your hands, into the vessel and enchant your potion. You may wish to repeat your name several times so that you really connect with this energy.

Anoint the top of your head, your throat, heart, wrists and the soles of your feet with the potion. As you do this, say the words: 'I can. I can. I can.'

Step into your power, acknowledging that you are more than capable and deserving of any opportunities that come your way. This potion can be charged up under a Full Moon for extra 'oomph'.

HEART HEALING OIL

Credit where credit's due, your heart is amazing. Not only does it keep you alive, it generates powerful, loving energy. However many times it may get broken, it always heals, and with a healed heart often comes deep wisdom.

Use this spell to send healing energy to a broken heart or to honour your heart for the healing that has been done. This potion can also be used to bless your heartbeat and send magical, heartfelt healing energy to loved ones, the universe and beyond.

If you are reading this and your heart is currently broken: I promise you it will feel better soon. It might not feel like it now, but I promise it will.

You will need:

60ml (2fl oz) carrier oil of your choice

15 drops of rose essential oil

10 drops of cardamon essential oil

a glass jar or potion bottle

Blend the oils in a clockwise direction. As you do this, think of someone you love and who loves you back. Feel the energy of this love flowing through your body and out of your hands into the potion.

Take a few drops of the potion, rub it between your hands and place your hands on your heart. Connect to the beat of your heart and begin gently massaging, feeling the connection to your heart's energy. Close your eyes and visualise a little face on your beating heart; see the little face smile at you and give it a smile back. Feel the warmth and loving energy of the potion travelling through your body. As you do this, know that deep healing is happening and great wisdom is incoming.

GREEN GODDESS ORGAN ELIXIR

You will need:
1 extra-large handful of spinach
1 thumb of fresh ginger
1 handful of fresh coriander
1 handful of fresh parsley
juice of 1 lemon
a large glass of coconut water

Big shout out to our organs! Doing their thing and working 24/7 behind the scenes. Let's send them some extra love with a body-boosting green juice.

Blitz all the ingredients in a blender until smooth. Drink up and visualise the green goodness sending vitality to your organs. Tell them how much you love them and thank them for all they do.

MAGICAL FOOTSTEPS

You will need:
1 cup sea salt, Himalayan
  or Epsom salts
  (or a mix of all of them)
1 cup coconut oil
10 drops of peppermint
  oil
5 drops of thyme
  essential oil

Use this spell to give you the courage to walk your own path and not follow in anyone else's footsteps.

―――――――

Blend the ingredients together and give your feet a scrub. As you do this, visualise all the places that you would like to walk to: all the new, uncharted territory, and bless them with courage for all the places they will take you.

'ENOUGH ALREADY' OIL FOR BODY POWER

This is a potion to acknowledge that you have had 'enough already' of giving your body a hard time! Enough of hearing your inner critic talk badly about your body. Enough of carrying the 'shame' of stretch marks, scars, fleshy bits or anything else you have been giving yourself a hard time about.

You can find hundreds of search results online showing you how to get rid of 'bingo wings' or 'muffin tops', yet searches of how to accept yourself and love these parts of your body seem to be few and far between.

Let's change that narrative. Use this potion to honour the parts of you that you have been conditioned into believing you have to hide. Create this oil with compassion and unconditional love for your unique and one-of-a-kind body. Use it to bring conscious awareness to the limited cultural expectations of what 'attractive' is deemed to be.

You will need:
100ml (3¾ fl oz) carrier oil (almond, apricot kernel, jojoba or coconut oil would be best)
15 drops of rosemary essential oil
10 drops of bergamot essential oil
5 drops of cinnamon essential oil
a glass jar or bottle

Blend the ingredients in a clockwise direction. As you blend them, feel bright, sparkly, golden light beaming in through the top of your head and out through your hands. Massage your body with this oil and repeat these affirmations:

'My body is perfect for me.
My body is unique to me.
I am comfortable in my skin.
I am happy and healthy.
I am beautiful.
I am smart.
I am love.
I am free.
All I need is within me right now.'

Continue to gently massage the parts of you that you have struggled to accept, telling them you love them. Kiss your fingertips and place them wherever needs a little kiss.

A REBIRTH TO REDEFINE YOUR DEFINITION OF BEAUTY

You will need:
a walnut
a hammer (or something
  with which to crush
  the walnut)
a clear quartz crystal
a yellow pouch or
  square of fabric and
  string

Use this spell to banish the confinements of how other people have defined beauty. Break away from conditioned stereotypes of what is supposed to be beautiful and find your own meaning.

————————

Hold the walnut between your hands and think about how your definition of beauty has been established by other people. Think about how many conversations you have had with your friends or yourself about your body and the things you would like to change about it. Think about where these thoughts have come from and how unfair they are. Think about all of your friends and the women in the world who have to abide by these patriarchal beauty standards.

Allow yourself to be angry about it and sit in that fury. Let this rage transit through your hands and into the walnut. When it feels right, smash the walnut with the hammer.

Enjoy the sense of relief that you have a new awareness and a new way to redefine your version of beauty.

When you feel ready, add the smashed walnut and the clear quartz crystal to your yellow pouch, or wrap it in a square of fabric, bring all of the corners together and tie with some string.

Carry the pouch around with you for a moon cycle, and every time you look at it, reflect on what it represents. When the moon cycle is complete, place it in a plant pot with a flourishing plant (indoor or outdoor is fine).

Fun fact: In magic, walnuts represent discernment as the means to develop awareness and understanding prior to taking action.

A RADICAL SPELL
FOR SELF-LOVE
FROM WITHIN

We pray to gurus and have images of gods
and goddesses on our altars, but how about
taking a moment to worship yourself! Here
is a ritual to honour yourself and everything
that you have been through, the highs and
the lows and everything in between.

Use this spell to awaken and activate
unconditional love for yourself.

You will need:
a picture of yourself
2 yellow candles
frankincense resin
  (optional)
fresh flowers and herbs
  of your choice
money (this could be
  coins or paper money)
your favourite crystals
a pink pouch

Create an altar around your picture. Stare deeply into your own eyes in the picture and tell yourself that you love you. Focus on what you have done that has been kind towards yourself recently, and acknowledge areas where you have been hard on yourself.

Lovingly acknowledge everything that you have survived and all that you have achieved.

If you wish to go deeper, burn some frankincense and call on a nurturing voice. Allow this voice to talk to you with words of unconditional love. If you like, give this voice a name, and maybe visualise what they might look like (you can allow yourself to go crazy with your imagination here!). Hear this nurturing voice pay you all the compliments you need to hear. Write them down or speak them out loud to your picture.

When this spell is complete, you may wish to place the coins and the flowers or herbs in a pink pouch and keep it in your bag, or hang it on a door, window or somewhere you will see it everyday so you are reminded of the messages that came through when doing this ritual.

A SPELL TO HONOUR YOUR OWN PATH AND LIVE LIFE YOUR WAY

You will need:
bay leaves
a pen
a handful of basil
a handful of rose petals
a handful of rosemary
a bowl
an emerald crystal
a glass jar

Use this spell to bless your own personal path. What dreams do you have for your future that are just for you?

———————

On the bay leaves, write down the dreams and wishes you hope to bless your path with. Blend the rest of the ingredients together and add them to a bowl with the emerald crystal in the centre. Burn the bay leaves over the bowl, and as each one burns, allow the ash to fall on the herbs in the bowl. As you burn them, speak your wishes out loud, visualise them, feel them and believe them.

Remember this spell is about wishes just for your path and no one else's. These wishes are just for you.

Sprinkle a handful or two of the mixture on the path to your home, leave a little bowl of it by your front door and keep some in your pocket to sprinkle on your path when you go for a walk. Store the leftovers in a jar and keep on your altar next to a thriving plant.

Continue to sprinkle it on your path over the next moon cycle, to remind you of your wishes.

BANISH MILESTONES

You will need:
21 drops of bergamot
  essential oil
a few pinches of lavender
a yellow candle
fennel or star anise
  herbal tea

There is a tremendous pressure to meet certain 'life milestones', such as finding a partner, buying a house or having children. We are all so different, yet societal expectations can make you feel as if these boxes must be ticked at certain points in your life, and if you aren't doing so, you can be made to feel like a failure.

Remember that it is okay to go at your own pace, make your own choices and do things when they feel right for you; what is right for other people may not bring you happiness. Use this spell to ignore these pressures and summon the energy to trust the process, knowing that when you do so, the next stage will unveil itself.

———

Blend the lavender and bergamot essential oil together and anoint the candle (you can do this by tipping the anointing potion onto a plate and rolling the candle in it). Light the candle and say the words:

'Societal pressures are not for me.
I am free and I can see
An abundance of opportunity.
I trust the universe will guide me"

Make a cup of herbal tea (fennel or star anise, or combine the two), and as you sip it, gaze at the candle's flame and call in your trailblazer energy, knowing that you are creating a new path and a new way of living for those who come after you.

A SPELL TO BANISH COMPARISON

You will need:
12 drops of lavender
  essential oil
1 tsp thyme
salt
a blue candle
a pen and paper
1 bay leaf

Comparing yourself to people around you – or people you don't know on social media – is a low vibrational energy blocker. Whether it's comparing bodies, love lives, social lives, holidays, families or finances, when we spend time comparing ourselves to others we give away our personal power. This can create a very lonely place and can trigger anxiety and fear, which can be completely paralysing.

Use this spell to summon your personal power and banish the comparison cycle.

———————

Blend the lavender oil and thyme together and anoint the candle with this blend. Create a ring of salt around the base of the candle, then light the candle.

As you gently gaze at the candle, allow yourself to hear the voice of comparison. Let it talk to you and allow it to say its worst, knowing that this is the last you will be hearing of it! As it continues to talk to you, connect to the awareness that this voice is not you and trust that your soul would never talk to you in this way.

On a piece of paper, write out one of the things that this voice is saying to you. Now tune in to a nurturing voice and hear it telling you, 'You are enough.'

Take the message from the negative voice and burn it on the flame of the candle.

Write on the bay leaf, in capital letters, 'I AM ENOUGH.' Light it with the candle flame and repeat the mantra 'I am enough' nine times. Each time you say it, allow these powerful words to be absorbed by all the cells in your body.

As the candle continues to burn, make a promise that future comparisons will be made only to compare your current self to your past self. Mentally list all your personal growth and the personal achievements that have happened in your own life.

A SPELL TO HONOUR BEING SINGLE

This isn't so much of a spell but more of a magical quest: indulge yourself, romance yourself and take yourself on a date.

This is a personal ritual that has guided me through my life during times of being single and it really is a liberating experience. Why wait for someone to romance you when you can romance yourself?

Switch the narrative and tune in to the empowering energy of being completely independent.

A ritual – any ritual – can be a magical practice, and dating yourself truly is. So make a date in your diary, plan your outfit and plan what you are going to do. Buy yourself flowers, eat your favourite meal, pleasure yourself in every single way possible, indulge yourself, romance yourself, enjoy your own company. Find something that you enjoy doing just for you.

FORTUNE FAVOURS
THE BOLD BLESSING

You will need:
1 pinch of marjoram
1 pinch of thyme
1 pinch of lavender
1 charcoal disk

Use this incense to awaken the trailblazer within. Allow it to bring you courage to do things your way, to banish the 'life script' imposed upon you.

———————

Mix these herbs together in a clockwise direction in a pestle and mortar. Place the mixed herbs on some hot coal (see instructions on page 11) and bathe your body in the smoke.

Bless your body with the smoke. Use it to charge up your energy and to bring courage and vitality to your auric field.

A SPELL TO MARRY YOURSELF

You are the person you have to spend the rest of your life with, in sickness and in health, for richer or poorer, until your soul leaves your body. You need to learn to rely on yourself and count on yourself. Of course, friends, family and lovers may come and go, but you are with you always, evolving, growing and learning. This is a spell to commit to yourself, a declaration of true self-compassion, a promise that you will always honour yourself and give yourself the self-respect that you deserve.

This ritual can be done alone, in front of friends or as a group ceremony.

You will need:
a generous handful of
  rose petals
a piece of jewellery
  (this can be something
  that you treat yourself
  to, or a piece that you
  already own – if it is a
  piece that you already
  own, give it a little
  cleanse in some salt
  water or a cleansing
  smoke first, see page
  108).
2 cinnamon sticks
pink thread

Arrange an altar and add a circle of rose petals;
place the piece of jewellery in the centre.

Begin by creating some vows for yourself, promises
that you wish to keep. Tie the cinnamon sticks
together with the pink thread, and with each knot
say one of your vows out loud.

Light one end of the cinnamon stick bundle and
bless the jewellery with the smoke. As you do
this, think of all the promises you wish to make
to yourself.

When it feels right, put the piece of jewellery on
and continue to burn the cinnamon and bless
the jewellery.

Wear the jewellery every day for a moon cycle,
and every time you look at it, remind yourself of
your commitment to yourself. Continue to burn
the cinnamon sticks and bless the jewellery as
often as you like.

A SPELL TO HONOUR YOUR SHADOW AND HEAL YOUR SHAME

You will need:
rosemary (dried or
  fresh, both will work)
sage essential oil
a purple candle
a promise of total self-
  compassion
100% honesty
a nurturing inner
  dialogue
pen and paper

Shadow work is inner alchemy; it isn't easy, but it is where the most transformational and powerful energy shifts happen. It is all about connecting to the unseen parts of ourselves, the parts where we might feel shame, anger, jealousy or guilt. It's about tuning in to the dark depths of ourselves then turning it to light.

This kind of self-exploration is an ongoing practice and is challenging, but I promise it is worth it as the deep energy shifts that take place when you connect to your shadow can be life-changing. Shadow work requires you to be completely honest with yourself, which is why it can be so difficult.

Blend the rosemary and sage essential oil and anoint the candle (the easiest way to do this is by rolling the candle in the blend on a plate).

Create a protective circle and/or call in your spirit guides for protection (see page 13). Start by examining thoughts in your mind. You can work through things that have triggered you, annoyed you, created a dramatic reaction, irritated you or any areas where you might have felt resistance or felt not good enough.

Journal your thoughts, allowing yourself to see where your mind takes you, and as you do this, create a pros and cons list about yourself.

Allow yourself to really feel any emotions that surface, and explore where any beliefs and ideas come from.

Connect to any trauma that might come up, and remember to show yourself compassion as you do so.

Remember that not everything is going to be clear or will come up in just one session of exploring your shadow: this is an ongoing practice, one that you can do on a Dark Moon or, if you are feeling brave, on a Full Moon. Anything that is lurking in the shadows on a Full Moon will more often than not make itself seen, especially if you look for it.

When you feel like you have worked through a shadow, write it down and burn it. As it burns, repeat three times:

'The shadow within me,
I acknowledge thee.
And now it is time to set it free.
Thank you for the lesson,
But now it is time to welcome in new energy.'

Note: Sometimes this stuff can be intense to deal with on your own. There is no shame in connecting to a therapist to help you work through it.

A SPELL TO HONOUR A MISTAKE YOU HAVE MADE

Our failures and mistakes can often carry shame when in fact these are the moments in our life that can teach us our greatest lessons. These experiences act as powerful guides and teachers that create new paths and new life experiences. By recognising these moments, addressing them and honouring them through a ritual, we can create a powerful energetic acknowledgement that will shift you into a frequency of wisdom and healing.

You will need:
pen and paper
a handful of fresh
  rosemary
an envelope
1 clear crystal (selenite
  or a clear quartz)

Draw a line down the centre of the paper, and on one side of the line write out your mistake. On the other side, write out a lesson that you have learned from this mistake.

When you have spent some time reflecting on what you have written, sprinkle the rosemary over the paper and add it all to an envelope.

Burn the envelope and bathe the crystal in the smoke. Place the crystal somewhere facing west – the direction of water – to represent the cleansing that has taken place. On a Dark Moon you could also bury this crystal or throw it in a river.

Witches Need Spells

Witches Need Money

Financial independence is important for BWE.
Not having to rely on anyone, not having to feel
guilty or having any shame around money are
empowering positions to be in. These spells help
you truly become the master of your money.

MONEY POWDER

You will need:
3 pinches of basil
3 pinches of mint
1 cinnamon stick
3 pinches of nutmeg
3 pinches of sugar
7 coins (silver or gold, not copper)
a clear glass jar

Use this spell to bring financial security into your life.

———

Place the herbs, spices and sugar in a pestle and mortar. As you add the ingredients, thank each pinch you add for the money they are going to bring you.

Blend the spell in a clockwise direction. As you do this, repeat the incantation:

'Magic herbs I blend thee.
Magic spell bring money to me,
To bring me financial security.
No set limit is coming to me,
This or better,
So mote it be.'

Transfer the magical blend and the coins to the glass jar. It is important that the jar has been cleansed first – to do this, wash it in salt water or cleanse it by burning some sage or rosemary and filling it up with the smoke.

Spend some time gazing at the jar and visualising financial freedom, and feel this energy blessing the spell.

Sprinkle the money powder in your purse, your pockets and over the entrance to your home.

MONEY MAGNETISM

You will need:
yellow flowers (this could
  be chamomile, calendula
  or a blend of both)
money and/or cheques
1 lodestone crystal
iron filings
green pouch (optional)

Lodestones are my favourite crystals for manifesting with, especially when casting money spells. See them as little pets, give them a name, tell them what you want and 'feed' them with iron filings on a regular basis and see how hard they work for you.

———————

Create a circle with the flowers and place some money in the centre. Place the lodestone crystal in the centre of the circle, on top of the money, and sprinkle some of the iron shavings onto it (this is known as 'feeding').

Continue to 'feed' the lodestone with the iron filings every day. As you do so, visualise money magnetising towards you, just as the iron filings are drawn to the lodestone.

You can either keep this on your altar or, after seven days of feeding, add the lodestone and money to a green pouch and continue to feed it as and when. You can also charge this up beneath a full Moon.

'GET THE JOB'
SPELL

You will need:
1 pinch of cinnamon
1 pinch of basil
1 pinch of thyme
50ml of a carrier oil of
  your choice
a bay leaf

Call on your spirit guides for assistance, whether it's to ace a job interview or bring luck to an important work meeting.

———

Blend the ingredients together. As you do so, imagine the meeting or interview going well, see yourself charm them and them smiling and being impressed by you.

Write 'thank you' on your bay leaf and call out to your spiritual team. (Your spiritual team is made up of your spirit guides, loved ones who are watching over you, pets who have passed over and other ancestors.) Burn the bay leaf and bless the potion with the smoke. Leave the potion uncovered in a bowl overnight, and ask your spiritual team to connect with the potion as you sleep.

In the morning, transfer the potion to a glass bottle or jar. When you go to your interview or meeting, anoint the palms of your hands with the potion before you shake anyone's hand, and if possible, rub a drop on a door on the way into the building.

Imagine your entire spiritual team is with you, and know that during your meeting your spiritual team is there schmoozing and networking with everyone else's spiritual teams for you.

GREEN CANDLE
MONEY SPELL

You will need:
9 drops of patchouli
  essential oil
9 drops of orange
  essential oil
1 pinch of dried
  chamomile
1 pinch of dried basil
1 green candle
7 coins (gold, silver
  or both)
7 bay leaves

This is a money and prosperity spell to draw money to your home and your business. This spell is to be performed over seven nights and will be most potent over a New Moon/Waxing Moon phase.

To make the anointing potion, blend the patchouli and orange essential oils with the chamomile and basil leaves.

Anoint your candle with the anointing potion. Do this by tipping the anointing potion onto a plate and rolling the candle in it. Place the candle in the centre of a plate or a tray (you may need to hold a flame to the base of the candle and melt it a little so that it sticks). Surround the candle with gold and silver coins and light it.

On one of the bay leaves, write out the amount of money you wish this spell to bring you – think big and don't hold back on the amount! Light the bay leaf with the candle's flame and allow the ash to fall around the base of the candle (you might want to hold the bay leaf with some tongs so you don't burn your fingers).

Continue to stare at the flame and visualise checking your bank balance and seeing the amount of money you are manifesting in your account.

Feel the emotions that you will feel when you see this amount, notice where you feel it in your body and hold onto this feeling so that you can revisit and tune in to it anytime. Spend some time with the candle, imagining all the things you can do with the money when it comes to you.

When it feels right, blow out the candle, then continue to relight the candle over the next six nights, each time writing the amount of money you want on a bay leaf and burning it over the candle.

When the spell is finished, carry the coins around in your purse.

A SPELL FOR SUCCESS IN YOUR BUSINESS

You will need:
a picture of yourself
a strand of your hair
your business card, or
  your business's name
  written on a piece
  of paper
a clear glass jar
1 pinch of basil
1 thumb of ginger
1 pinch of nutmeg
1 pinch of allspice
1 pinch of chamomile
1 cinnamon stick
1 citrine crystal

Use this spell to bless and bring prosperity to your business. Use it to inspire and conjure new opportunities, contracts and collaborations.

———————

Start with adding your picture, the strand of hair and business card to the jar. Then add all the herbs, spices and citrine crystal.

As you are adding everything to the jar, imagine all the success that is coming to your business. Keep a pen and paper handy, as it is likely that ideas of how to make your business flow and grow will pop into your head.

Spend some time hanging out with the spell and writing down your goals and all the successes you wish for. Write them either as a list, or write them in past tense as if they have already come true. Add this list to the spell jar.

Place your jar facing east and call on the energy of this direction to welcome visions of abundance. Ask out loud for the spirits of the east to shower your spell with magical blessings.

BANISHING DEBT

You will need:

1 lemon rind
1 garlic clove, unpeeled
1 tsp cayenne pepper
9 drops of rosemary
  essential oil
30ml (1fl oz) carrier oil
  (2 tbsp)
a tealight candle for
  each of your debts
debt letters, bills or
  the amount of your
  debts written out on
  separate pieces
  of paper
1 cup salt

While performing this spell, be conscious of any debt-banishing ideas. Remember that magic works in mysterious ways, so keep an ear out for any opportunities that might come your way to help you clear your debt.

Blend the lemon rind, garlic and cayenne pepper and oils in an anti-clockwise direction in a pestle and mortar. Create a circle with the salt, place the tealights in the centre and anoint each of the candles with the banishing oil by putting a few drops on the top.

Lights the tealights and burn each of the bills or pieces of paper. As the tealights burn, feel the relief of the debt dissolving. Sit with the tealights until they have burned out. While the spell is working, pay attention to any dreams, ideas, conversations and opportunities that might come your way to help relieve the debt.

GENERATIONAL MONEY CORD-CUTTING

You will need:
1 pinch of rosemary
1 pinch of rue
1 pinch of sage
1 pinch of myrrh
1 pinch of frankincense
  resin
1 charcoal disk
a chain that is easy to
  break (if you can't find
  a chain, you can do
  this spell with a
  paper chain)
black cloth and black
  thread

**For a cleansing bath
or scrub:**
3 cups sea salt
juice of 1 lemon
7 drops of lavender
  essential oil
1 cup carrier oil
  (optional)

We can carry a lot of negative stories of financial hardship and negative belief systems in our bloodlines. Sometimes these patterns are learned or inherited, and sometimes they are from our own past lives.

Use this spell to clear this energy; let the spirits and ancestors who hang around you know that you are changing the story of your family's relationship to money.

———————

Blend all the herbs and resins in a pestle and mortar, stirring in an anti-clockwise direction for banishing power.

Put a pinch of the banishing blend on some hot coal (see page 11). Hold the chain over the smoke and visualise the link in the centre of the chain representing you, and that the links attached on both sides are representing past lives and generations before you. Spend some time looking at all of the links and designating each of them to past lives, old soul contracts and generational setbacks, scripts and stories.

When it feels right and you are ready to break away, hold the chain in the smoke and break it.

As you break it, repeat this chant three times:

'This ends here and now with me.
These generational ties no longer serve me.
Stories, scripts and contracts of the past,
I break this chain and banish thee.
Thank you universe, so mote it be.'

Feel the freedom of this breaking. Place the chain and the remaining blend in black cloth and tie the top with some black thread, tying it in three tight knots.

Dispose of this far away from your house, either by burying it somewhere where nothing grows or chucking it in a bin that belongs to someone else. Try to make sure that the place of disposal isn't somewhere you walk past often.

A cleansing bath or shower is recommended for renewal after performing a powerful banishing spell like this. To do so, mix the sea salt, lemon juice and lavender essential oil and add to a bath. If you don't have a bath, blend with a cup of carrier oil and use it as a body scrub in the shower.

Note: This spell can also be used for any generational cord-cutting, not just financial.

MONEY
PORTAL

You will need:
1 black candle
pen and paper
1 white candle

Sometimes the portals we use to receive can get blocked, and the only way to clear these is to go deep and connect with our shadow.

Use this spell to recognise and connect to money patterns, beliefs and opinions, clear them, and open up the portal to allow you to receive financial abundance.

This is a shadow-working spell, and with these types of spell it is important that you give yourself some time before and after to process what comes up and what needs clearing. You can start with a bath, meditation or – even better – both! And afterwards make a promise that your phone or any other electronics will stay switched off for at least an hour.

I would recommend using small altar candles for these types of spells as their burn time is usually around an hour.

Start by lighting the black candle and promising to honour your shadow in order to clear it. On your piece of paper, answer the following questions:

1. What is your opinion of money?
2. What does money mean to you?
3. What do you think of people with money?
4. What was your family's relationship with money when you were growing up?
5. Does money make you feel stressed?
6. Does money make you feel shame?
7. What is your first memory of money?

Remember to give yourself some time to answer these questions; they can be incredibly insightful so you want to give yourself time to process. Know that as the candle burns and you answer questions, acknowledging these feelings is helping to unlock the portal.

When you have written everything out, burn it with the flame from the black candle.

As it burns, repeat this chant:
'I am free of these financial burdens.'

Repeat it as many times as you like to connect with this powerful energy shift.

Now light the white candle from the black candle's flame. As you do so, say the words:
'Financial abundance is my birthright.'

Again, repeat this chant loudly and clearly as many times as you like to connect to this abundant energy.

On another piece of paper, write a love letter to money. Welcome it and write how much you love it. Include opposite responses to all your shadow feelings, e.g. how amazing your memories of money are, how it has never stressed you out and how it brings calm and feelings of abundance, freedom and security.

Burn this paper with the flame of the white candle and know that the smoke is sending out a powerful message to the universe and creating a shift in your financial frequency. Your money portal is now clear and you are ready to receive.

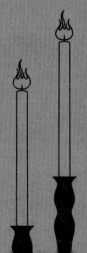

Witches
Need Courage

MIRROR SPELL

You will need:
a small hand mirror
salt water or sage
  (optional)
the most over-the-top
  flower you can find
a red jasper crystal
a bowl of water

Enchant a mirror with powerful sunlight to bring courage and confidence.

———————

Start by cleaning the mirror; you can choose to wash it with salt water or burn sage over it. Add the flower and red jasper crystal to the bowl of water, put your fingertips in the water and think of a time you did something that took courage.

Spend some time calling in the power of this memory and feeling the energy travel through your body, through your fingertips and into the water. When you feel like you have charged the water with your energy, place the mirror in the bowl and leave it to soak up sunlight (ideally this will be when the sun is at its strongest, around noon).

When you remove the mirror, dry it with a clean cloth. Your mirror is now blessed. Stare at your reflection and charge yourself up with courage.

COURAGE CHARM

You will need:
1 carnelian crystal
1 pinch of basil
1 pinch of thyme
a square of orange fabric
a few drops of orange
  essential oil
red string

This is a charm to invoke the courage to handle anything that comes your way. It's also super effective at allowing yourself to be seen, such as when public speaking or having difficult conversations.

Add the carnelian crystal, basil and thyme to the centre of the fabric square and sprinkle over a few drops of the orange essential oil.

Gather all the corners of the square together and tie with the red string.

As you tie the first knot, say, 'I have courage.'

As you tie the second knot, say, 'I am confident.'

As you tie the third knot, say, 'I am brave.'

Carry the charm with you and sniff when you need an extra boost of courage.

COURAGE TO BREAK AWAY FROM A TOXIC RELATIONSHIP

You will need:
5 juniper berries
5 black peppercorns
juice of 1 lemon
1 orange candle
pen and paper

For the tea (1 cup):
5 cloves
juice of half a lemon
5ml (0.2fl oz) mugwort
  (1 tsp)

There comes a time in a toxic relationship when a spell is needed to summon the courage to say 'enough is enough'. Honouring your feelings and leaving is a huge act of self-love. As difficult as it is to walk away, you know you can no longer accept disrespectful behaviour or ignore the red flags; you need to be true to yourself.

Use this spell to summon the courage to walk away from a bad relationship.

Crush the juniper berries and peppercorns, then blend them with the lemon juice. Anoint the orange candle (you can do this by tipping the anointing potion onto a plate and rolling the candle in it), and as you anoint the candle ask it to remind you why you must leave, that you are worth more than this treatment and that you are worthy of a respectful, loving relationship.

Brew your tea, and as the candle burns, recount why you must leave, write it down and burn in with the candle's flame.

Continue to gaze at the flame and sip the tea, calling for it to bring you psychic visions of empowerment. See yourself living a life without toxicity, and set some intentions on how you would like things in your future to be.

Of course, leaving isn't always so easy. If this is the case, use this spell to call in signs and alignments for assistance to help you move on.

Witches
Need Luck

LUCKY FUTURE

You will need:
1 tsp cinnamon
1 tsp allspice
7 mint leaves
a key
a stand of your hair
a green square of fabric
  or a green pouch
  (a neutral pouch would
  also work)

Use this spell to bring luck to your life and open routes to lucky opportunities.

––––––––––

Add all the ingredients to the centre of the cloth or the pouch. Hold it in both hands and say:

'I call on the magical power of this key
To unlock multiple blessings for me.
I welcome luck of the highest kind,
Summoning magic for me to find.
Abundance is coming to me
As I enter this powerful frequency.
This or better come to me.
Thank you universe,
So mote it be.'

EVERYTHING LUCKY OIL

You will need:
1 tsp allspice
1 tsp ground nutmeg
1 tsp dried basil
9 drops of orange
  essential oil
2 cups water
a spritzer bottle

Invite lucky blessings to literally everything with this oil. As it cooks it will fill and bless your home with its lucky scent. Use it to anoint the entrance to your house, your body, keys, candles, laptop and anything else you wish to be blessed with this potion.

———————

Add the ingredients to a pot and gently simmer over a low heat. As the potion heats up, notice its aroma of pure abundance filling your home.

Look around you and write out a list of all the abundance you have around you.

Strain the spell into a spritzer bottle and spray around your house and in your aura.

ULTIMATE
LUCK JAR

You will need:
a piece of paper with
  your birth number
a small handful of
  chamomile
a citrine crystal
a piece of gold or silver
  jewellery
a clear glass jar
1 yellow candle
9 drops of orange
  essential oil

Combining magic with numerology is a powerful way to connect magic directly to you. Bring blessings to your birth number with this luck spell.

———————

Firstly, to calculate your birth number, add all the numbers from your birth date together to get a single number. For example, 11th November 1980 would be 1+1+1+1+9+8+0=22, then 2+2=4.

Add the chamomile, crystal and jewellery to the jar, then burn the paper with your birth number and add the ashes to the jar, too. Close the jar, anoint the candle with the orange essential oil and fix the candle to the lid of the jar by heating the base of the candle and securing it to the lid. Place this facing east.

Light the candle and let it burn down – you can choose to do this in one sitting or relight the candle over several nights. If you want to perform this over several nights, I recommend doing this spell on a New Moon.

GOOD LUCK BLESSING

You will need:
frankincense
rose petals
basil
cinnamon
1 charcoal disk
a piece of jewellery that
  you wear every day

A good luck charm to carry around with you and inspire luck, wherever you are.

―――――――――

Blend the frankincense, petals, herbs and spices in a clockwise direction in a pestle and mortar, then add a pinch of the spell over the hot coal (see page 11).

Bathe your chosen piece of jewellery in the smoke. As the smoke travels know that it is sending a powerful signal out to the universe to bring you luck.

Every day, when you look at the piece of jewellery, ask it to guide you to where the luck is that day.

WITCHES MANIFEST

You will need:
1 bay leaf
pen and paper
1 pinch of basil
9 drops of patchouli
   essential oil
1 green candle
2 lodestone crystals
   (or magnets)
iron filings

Perform this spell on a New Moon when setting your intentions and manifesting a specific outcome.

———————

On the bay leaf write what you are manifesting – this could just be a word or two, or a symbol. Then, add it to the mix and blend it with the basil and patchouli oil. Anoint the candle with this blend (you can tip the anointing potion onto a plate and roll the candle in it).

Light your candle and write out your intentions on a piece of paper. Gaze into the flame while holding a lodestone in each hand. Visualise everything that you are manifesting coming true and notice your vibrational frequency shift into the frequency of receiving. When you feel the spell is complete, place the crystals in the centre of your written-out intentions.

Anoint the corners of the paper with any remnants of the anointing potion. Fold the paper and continue to feed the lodestones with the iron filings (see Money Magnetism Spell on page 90 for how to feed them).

Witches Need Love

Love spells are one of the oldest and most legendary forms of magic, but there are some important things to remember when casting love spells.

Before any love spell, always think about what it is that you want from a person in a relationship, then give it to yourself first.

Avoid performing a love spell when you have a broken heart; I promise you this can get messy and the energy can get very confusing.

Don't cast a love spell when you are feeling pessimistic about love or not feeling fully in your power, as it won't connect with the right energy.

And, most importantly, never cast a love spell on someone without their permission - it is highly unethical! Imagine how you would feel if you found out you were dating someone and it wasn't of your own free will.

LOVE COME
TO ME SPELL

You will need:
2 pink candles
rose quartz crystal
dried flowers and herbs
1 bay leaf
pink velvet pouch

Note: It would be
highly unethical to
use this spell to bind
someone specific to
you. Instead, use this
spell to call in the
best possible love
towards you.

To call love into your life.

To create your altar, place both candles next to
each other with the crystal between them (to
secure the candles to a plate or tray, hold a flame
to the base of the candles and melt the wax).
Sprinkle the dried flowers and herbs around the
base of the candles and light them.

Write the word 'love' on the bay leaf, light it and
burn it over the candles (you may want to use some
tongs to hold the bay leaf so that you don't burn
your fingers).

Allow the ash from the bay leaf to fall on your
altar. As the candles burn, write out a list of all the
things you love about yourself to acknowledge
how loveable you are and to let your future lover
know what a catch you are. Burn the candles in one
sitting (it should take about an hour). Remember,
never leave candles unattended, so if you need to
leave the spell blow out the candles and re-light
when you return.

When the candles have burnt down, remove the
crystal, give it a kiss and place it in the pouch. Take
two pinches of herbs from your altar dressing and
sprinkle them into the pouch. Carry the pouch with
you, leave it by your bed or by a window (whatever
feels right).

SEND ME A SIGN

You will need:
a bowl of water
a rose quartz crystal
rose petals
a piece of string or
  ribbon
a ring (a simple band
  will work best)

Sometimes you need a sign to know if your love or crush is thinking about you. This spell is especially helpful if you have experienced being ghosted.

Add the rose quartz crystal to the bowl of water. Surround the bowl with rose petals and put the ribbon or string through the ring to create a pendulum.

Swing the pendulum over the bowl, say your name out loud three times, then say the name of who you are wondering about three times. As you say the name, allow the ring to tap the bowl.

Wear the pendulum, with the ring touching your heart, for an entire moon cycle. You may repeat this spell once a week if you desire. If you haven't had a response during the cycle, it is time to move on.

A SPELL TO FORGET YOUR EX

You will need:
a picture of your ex, an
  item of their clothing or
  a piece of paper with
  their full name written
  out 3 times
the root of a dead plant
black fabric or a black
  bag
black string

Focusing energy on your ex can be consuming – you want to move on, but you can't stop thinking about them. Use this spell to say goodbye, and know that when you do this, you are creating energetic space in your heart to welcome in new fresh energy and experiences.

———————

Place the picture, clothing or paper in the black cloth or bag and add the dead root. Scream, cry and/or swear into the bag . . . let it all out!

Gather the corners of the cloth or bag and tie tightly with string. Dispose of it in a bin far away from your house.

A SPELL TO GET BACK WITH YOUR EX

I am sorry to lure you in with this heading, but there is no such thing.

Over the years I have received countless emails from people asking me to perform a spell to get their ex back. They often mention how badly behaved their ex was. My standard response is that it would be highly unethical to perform a spell like this against someone's free will. Just imagine how you would feel if you found out you were bound to someone because they had put a spell on you! And secondly, let's not waste magic on someone who didn't treat you well (I'm presuming they didn't). Let's focus magic on loving yourself first and then manifesting a trustworthy, respectful, intimate lover instead, one who returns your calls and treats you with respect!

CUTTING AWAY AN EX

You will need:
a black candle
pen and paper
scissors
a house plant
a clear quartz crystal

This spell can be used for exes, people you no longer want in your life or situations you wish to break away from.

———————

Light the black candle.

Draw a line down the middle of the piece of paper, writing your name on one side and your ex's name on the other. Cut down the line in the middle of the paper

Burn the piece of paper with your ex's name on it and flush the ashes down the toilet.

Place the piece of paper with your name on the soil of a plant pot, and place the clear quartz crystal on top of the piece of paper.

Witches Need Protection

It is important to keep ourselves protected
and to practise good spiritual hygiene,
especially when practising magic. These
spells are designed with the intention of
keeping you energetically safe and banishing
negative vibes.

WITCH'S BOTTLE

You will need:

sage wand or sprig of
  rosemary
a small glass bottle or jar
a selection of sharp and
  rusty items – nails, bent
  pins, razor blades and
  broken glass
salt
urine (must be your
  own!)
a black candle

These bottles keep evil at bay and keep your home protected.

Start by cleansing the jar with sage or rosemary smoke. Fill the jar halfway up with all the sharp objects, then add a good layer of salt. Add some of your urine – this is to connect you to the jar and to ensure it is you who is protected.

Close the jar and seal it with the wax from the black candle. To do this, light the candle and allow the wax to drip around the seal.

Hide the jar somewhere on your property and out of the way. Ideally this would be buried outside the front of your house, but if you don't have a garden or if you live in an apartment, you can leave it at the back of the cupboard, under the kitchen sink or bury it in a plant pot.

PROTECTION POTION & CRYSTAL AMULET

You will need:
a glass jar
1 black tourmaline crystal
1 pinch of rue
1 pinch of thyme
10 drops of lavender
  essential oil
5 drops of frankincense
  essential oil
2 tbsp carrier oil
smoke of sage
a small pouch or a small
  piece of fabric and
  some string

Use this potion to protect and enchant the crystal; keep the crystal with you to shield you from negative energy.

───────

Add the crystal, herbs and oils to the jar, then fill the jar with the smoke of sage (this can either be from a sage wand or by burning some sage on hot coal).

Secure the lid on the jar and trap the smoke inside. Burn some more sage around the outside of the jar.

After seven nights remove the black tourmaline and place it in a fabric pouch to carry around with you. To make a pouch, use a square of fabric and pinch the corners together by tying it around the crystal and securing with three tight knots.

Save the oil and use it as a protection potion; this blend works really well to protect you while performing spells. To do so, anoint the outline of your body and third eye with the potion.

To recharge the black tourmaline, anoint it with the potion on a Full Moon.

BANISHING TOXICITY

You will need:
grated zest of 1 lemon
garlic skin
cayenne pepper
10 drops of rosemary
    essential oil
10 drops of sage
    essential oil
a picture or written
    description of what it
    is you wish to banish
black candle
paper bag (preferably
    black or brown)

This is a powerful cleanser for a total energetic reset.

———————

Blend the lemon zest, garlic skin, cayenne pepper and oils in an anti-clockwise direction to form a paste.

Write out a goodbye letter to whatever it is you wish to banish – if you need permission to get angry here, this is it! Feel free to use profanity and get your anger out. If you want, use a picture or visual representation of what it is you wish to banish.

Smear the paste all over your letter and/or images. Light the black candle and drip wax all over it.

As you cover what you are banishing with the wax, allow yourself to feel empowered – you are showing this toxic energy who is the boss, you are free.

When the black wax has covered the image/letter, place it in the paper bag. You can either burn the bag and its contents or dispose of it far away from where you live and throw it in someone else's bin.

This should be somewhere that isn't on a regular route you take and is best done on a Dark Moon, or waxing phase.

Outside
Sources

Sometimes us witches need to call in a little help from unseen energies. Spirit guides, goddesses, gods, spiritual muses, familiars (and unseen energies) can be beneficial to your magic, bringing inspiration, power, protection and deep wisdom to our spell-work and beyond.

Tapping into these outside sources can bring powerful assistance when manifesting, healing and divining. When working with these outside sources, it is important to be open to how these energies might connect with you. Keep your eyes peeled for signs that they will send you - they may visit you in your dreams or sometimes they might communicate via your inner voice.

Animal Energy and Familiars

Our furry, feathered and sometimes scaly friends often share a deep and intuitive connection with us. Whether we have sought them out or they have found their way to us, once that special bond is made it can inspire the purest, highest-grade unconditional love.

Sometimes these creatures can meet us mystically and become our familiars, assisting in spell-work, guiding us with their wisdom, protecting us and adding power to our magic.

It's important to remember not all our pets are our familiars - sometimes they are simply adorable little Earth angels who are here to make us smile, bring healing and be ridiculously cute! And sometimes young animals can grow into their familiar roles, but kittens just need to be kittens before they can take on such a role.

It is likely that you instinctively know when your
pet is your familiar, but there are signs if you are unsure.
For instance, they might always want to be involved when
you are practising magic, you may notice that their energy
levels are affected by the Moon's cycle, maybe you recognise
them from a past life or you feel a powerful energy shift
when they are hanging around you.

Sadly our familiars haven't always been adored and
celebrated this way. If we travel back to the Middle Ages,
during the witch trials, familiars were thought of as
demonic creatures, sent from the Devil to assist witches
with their magic.

It was believed that the familiars would feed on the witches,
suckling on their bodies and drinking their blood. When the
witches were on trial, the interrogation involved examining
their bodies and looking for what they called 'witches'
marks', such as scars or marks on the skin; they would claim
these were teeth marks from the familiars suckling blood.

Over the years, modern-day witches and Wiccans have
reclaimed familiars, recognising them as the powerful
energetic beings that they are. If you would like your pet to
become your familiar, it is always important that you ask
its permission first.

COMMUNICATING
WITH ANIMALS

You can communicate with your animal and connect to its energy by sitting close to them and mirroring their breathing.

Gently close your eyes and visualise yourself asking them if they want to be your familiar. Notice any change in energy you feel as their response – if you feel resistance then the answer is probably a 'no', or maybe it's a 'not right now'.

You can use this technique for communication with other animals too. Anytime you want to connect to, and communicate with, an animal on a deeper level, or have a message to give them, close your eyes and visualise whatever it is you wish to communicate with the animal. In my experience, they might not instantly get the message because sometimes communicating telepathically with animals can have a time delay.

Another way you can communicate with animals is with a pendulum. When they are relaxed, swing a pendulum over them and ask a yes or no question out loud. Start with some obvious questions that you know the answer to first, so that you know the pendulum is working.

You can also tune in to your familiar's psychic energy and get them to choose a tarot or oracle card for you. To do this, lay out your tarot deck or oracle cards and let your familiar choose some cards. They might choose by sniffing the card of choice, tapping it with their paw or flicking their tail over it.

FAMILIAR 'COME TO ME' SPELL

You will need:
1 tsp mugwort
1 tsp thyme
2 tsp chamomile
1 cinnamon stick

If you are without a familiar or intention to have a new pet in your life, complete this spell, then stay alert and remember your dream often so that your new animal can find its way to you.

Steep the ingredients in hot water, then strain into a cup before drinking. Drink this tea before you go to sleep. As you sip the tea, say the words:

'Magical familiar on your way to me,
Meet me in my dreams as I drink this tea.
Your forever home with me will be.
Come to me, so mote it be.'

As you continue to sip the tea, visualise the animal finding its way to you. Let your imagination create this story. As you drift off and fall asleep, continue to call in your familiar, knowing that you are sending out a signal in your dreams that they will hear.

INITIATING YOUR PET AS YOUR FAMILIAR

You will need:
rosemary essential oil
  or a sprig of fresh
  rosemary
a photo of your pet (it
  must be your own)
1 pinch of cinnamon
a handful of mugwort
a silk scarf, envelope
  or piece of
  parchment paper

Once you have asked your pet's permission and they have accepted to become your familiar, cast this spell to strengthen your psychic bond. This spell is most potent to perform on the third quarter/ Half Moon.

————————

Place a drop of rosemary essential oil on your third eye – or rub fresh rosemary leaves together to release their scent, inhale some and rub some on your third eye. Gently close your eyes and feel your third eye blink open. Spend some time meditating and visualising your pet in your mind's eye, then start thinking of their familiar name. This is a name that only you and they will share. It is to be a secret and you shouldn't tell anyone; the only time you can say it out loud to your familiar is when you are alone together.

When you have made a clear connection to the name and your pet approves, fold the picture of your pet in half and on one side write their given name and on the other side write their familiar name. Sprinkle the cinnamon and mugwort on the picture and wrap it in a silk scarf or piece of parchment paper. Sleep with it under your pillow for three nights.

You might notice that your pet is more affectionate or vocal during this time and you will be able to communicate telepathically. Spend time with them. If you visualise a message that you want to send them, they will usually respond fairly quickly.

WHISKERS AND CLAWS

Sometimes we will find our pets whiskers and claws in our homes - these can be used as powerful elements in spells.

Whiskers can be added to manifesting spells to speed things up and add potency. Sometimes when you find a whisker it can be a sign to create a spell using it.

Claws can be used in protection spells. If you find a claw, drop it by the entrance of your home for extra protection.

Note: claws and whiskers should only be used when they are found and never be removed from your pet.

PET PROTECTION

You will need:
1 pinch of dried rosemary
1 pinch of lavender
1 pinch of dried mint
your pet's collar, blanket
  or a clear quartz crystal
1 charcoal disc

Use this spell to keep your pet safe and bless it with protection; this spell can also be used to protect and send healing energy if a pet is unwell.

Blend the herbs together in a clockwise direction. Burn over some hot coal (see page 11 for directions), then bathe the collar, blanket or clear quartz crystal in the smoke. As you do this, visualise your familiar wearing the collar or using the blanket and see a bright blue light of protection surrounding them. If you are using a clear quartz crystal, bathe it in the smoke and visualise the blue light beaming from it and surrounding their body.

As you continue to bathe the item in the smoke, say the words:

'Smoke and herbs in the air,
Bless my familiar with love and care.
Keep them safe, keep them protected
and may our bond always be connected.'

CELEBRATION OF YOUR PET'S SOUL

You will need:
2 tbsp frankincense
2 tbsp myrrh
a small handful of rose
buds/petals
a small handful of
lavender
3 bay leaves
1 charcoal disc, for
burning

The pain of losing a pet or familiar can be devastating. It's important that you let yourself grieve; you are saying goodbye to a soul with which you have shared pure and unconditional love.

This ritual can be performed alone or with a gathering of anyone else who wants to say goodbye.

———————

Blend all the ingredients, except the coal, in a pestle and mortar, stirring in a clockwise direction.

Create an altar with your pet's body or their ashes, a photo of them, and surround them with fresh flowers, crystals and any of your pet's favourite toys. If you want to write any messages or a goodbye letter, you can add this too.

If you are in a group, have everyone sit around the altar and share a happy memory or a special moment they shared with your animal, and thank them for all the good times you shared.

As you do this, pass the incense around, then burn it on hot coal, knowing that the smoke is carrying the messages of love to your pet.

Keep a little of the incense and burn it anytime you are missing them and want to let them know you are thinking of them. After doing this, you may often hear footsteps, find white feathers or feel your pet's spirit rub against your ankles.

Auras

Our auras are an electromagnetic energy field that radiate around our bodies. This magical energy glows in a whole spectrum of colours, all corresponding to where you are at emotionally, physically and energetically.

These vibrant colours can be captured with a specially designed camera, but with a little practice it is possible to learn how to tune in and see this colourful energy field with your own eyes.

It is also possible to tune in to your own auric field and shift your energy by connecting to a colour that corresponds with the ritual that you are performing or energetic frequency you wish to step into.

Aura Colour Correspondences

RED: energetic, strongminded, passionate, creative, grounded, fearless.

PINK: open-hearted, generous, loving, nurturing, harmonious.

VIOLET: intellect, wisdom, spiritual awareness, creativity.

INDIGO: psychic, spiritually connected, in tune with higher self.

ORANGE: adventurous, considerate, thoughtful, a good friend, surrounded by good people.

YELLOW: creative, relaxed, friendly, happy, self-confident, playful.

BLUE: intuitive, spiritual, calm, spiritually protected, honest.

GREEN: good communicator, embraces personal growth, self-acceptance.

WHITE: balanced, empathetic, protected by spirit guides.

BLACK: carrying trauma, holding on to pain, closed mind, grieving.

HOW TO READ
YOUR AURA

This can be practised on yourself or someone else, but always remember to ask permission if you are reading someone else's. Note: it will work best against a white background.

Start by grounding yourself (see page 15). Give your third eye a few taps with your fingertips to awaken it, then close your eyes and take a few deep breaths. Spend some time connecting to your third eye, acknowledging the power that this magical energy portal holds.

Keeping your physical eyes closed, imagine your third eye blinking open and spend some time seeing through it. Observe your surroundings through it.

Now slowly begin to open your seeing eyes and squint or blink really fast for a moment so that you lose your regular focus. The goal here is to have blurred sight through your seeing eyes and to shift focus to your third eye.

Remember that this takes practice, so don't worry if you don't see everything right away.

Look at your own body, or someone else's. As you continue to gaze, start to examine the outline of the body. Focus on the area around the head and shoulders. You may start to see dots, or maybe a faint glow. If you see an assortment of colours, tune in to which one is the most prominent.

AURA SHIFTING

When we tune in to our aura energy and connect to the colour correspondence of the energy we wish to step into, it can have a positive effect on our energy levels, headspace and most importantly on our magic.

Tuning in to a specific colour's corresponding frequency can create empowering energetic shifts, almost like a magic cloak, surrounding you with the energy and power you wish to call in. This practice is especially empowering to call on before spell-work; it can be used to simply shift your energy if you are feeling blocked.

Start by thinking of the corresponding colour's values (see page 133) and what you would like to connect to. For example, you might be nervous about something and want to shift your energetic frequency to a more confident vibe.

Close your eyes and connect with the corresponding colour of the energy you wish to connect to. Start by seeing the colour in your mind's eye, and stay with the image of this colour for a short while. At first, it might shift and fade, so be sure to meditate on the colour until it is vivid.

When the colour feels clear in your mind, begin to imagine it travelling through your body, then feel it radiating around you, surrounding your entire body with an all-encompassing luminous glow. Now think about the energy that you want this auric colour to bring you; allow your aura to harness this energy and surround you with it.

This practice can also be reversed. To do this, see an image of yourself living with the energy and how that would feel, and as you do this, visualise whatever the corresponding colour is around you.

If you are finding it challenging to connect to this energy, try rubbing the palms of your hands together really fast for a minute – as you do this you are charging up an electromagnetic field. Feel the energy building up between your hands and focus on where you feel this energy. Look for a colour (this works best with a white/blank background, so I would suggest lying down on the floor and using the ceiling as your backdrop).

CALLING IN COLOURS

It is also possible to call your aura to you. To do this, close your eyes and hold the palms of your hands, facing you, about 15–20cm (6–8in) away. Very slowly move your palms back and forth, about 2cm (¾in) back and 2cm (¾in) forward, and as you do this you will start to feel an electromagnetic build up. When you can feel it, start to picture the corresponding auric colour, and continue to visualise the colour around you as you feel the energetic field surrounding you.

You can experiment with this and think of different memories that inspire different emotions and notice the colours change.

If you find visualising a colour challenging, try using a physical object that is the colour you want to work with. If you do this, have the physical object in front of you and stare at it, allowing your gaze to shift out of focus. When the colour is blurry, squint your eyes and call the colour towards you, as if you are summoning it with a beckoning gesture. Once you feel as if the colour is around you, go back to the first step.

Witch
Worship

Evoking Energy

It is possible to call in cosmic assistance from goddesses, gods, mythical creatures, spirits and magical beings. Harnessing energy this way can be powerful with all kinds of spell-work.

Whether it be calling in courage, clearing obstacles, bringing money, asking for guidance or protection, or just tapping into their essence for a little bit of empowerment and inspiration, they are a powerful force to have onside.

The main rule here is to never take advantage of this energy. Promise to be respectful and thankful, and always acknowledge when this energy has helped you.

There are many ways to connect to a deity; you might even find that sometimes they come and find you! They might appear in your dreams or meditations, maybe a specific tarot card keeps coming up in readings, or maybe an animal who is connected to a particular deity keeps showing up in your life.

You can also research and choose one. You might feel a connection to them because their story resonates with you, or you are working with a specific intention so you know exactly who is going to help you get the job done.

Human beings' and animals' energies can also be called in this way – I like to call them 'magical muses'. There might be someone or something you admire. Perhaps there is someone in the public eye who you have seen being interviewed, or maybe it's the way a friend has handled a situation, or it could even be wanting to tune in to the instincts of an animal. It is possible to tap into this energy via meditation, visualisation or create an altar for the energy that you wish to summon.

CONNECTING TO PEOPLE, ANIMALS AND SPIRITUAL MUSES

When connecting to a being's energy, start by thinking about the energy that you wish to conjure. Think about what it is you like about them, how they inspire you and what qualities you would like to harness.

Take some time to think about memories that you have of them, or maybe reflect on something that they have said.

Think about what they look like, how they hold themselves. Spend some time meditating on all of this to conjure their energy and get a good sense of who they are. Allow your unconscious mind to build a map of this person. Start to hear their voice and connect to their mind, and spend some time thinking the way they think and thinking how they might handle a situation.

Allow yourself to step into this energetic frequency and allow your subconscious self to embody this energy.

A personal favourite of mine is BFE (Big Feline Energy). Calling in BFE is always great for setting boundaries – cats are masters of setting clear boundaries, and they instantly let you know what is acceptable and what is not.

If you're feeling a little lacklustre and need to get your energy going, try tuning into some BPE (Big Puppy Energy). Think about how excited and curious puppies are about everything.

CONNECTING
TO DEITIES

Over the following pages are some rituals
to help you connect to some of my personal
favourite deities and goddesses, and some
tried-and-tested spells to connect with them.

HECATE (pronounced He-kah-tee)

Magic

The mother of all the witches, Hecate is said to be the goddess of magic and the underworld.

While Hecate is one of the most honoured Greek goddesses, her origin is also one of the most mysterious, with multiple stories of where she came from. She is often found at the crossroads between the living world and the underworld, always holding a key to gain access and a torch to guide the way.

If you want to invoke your BWE, Hecate is your goddess. Her archetypal energy is that of the mother, an energy that is strong and can handle anything. Her BWE sees beyond the veil, so if you work with her energy, be prepared to face some home truths and work through some of your shadow.

To tune up your magical frequency and embrace your BWE, you will need:

* mugwort
* lavender
* a key
* honey
* dark chocolate
* candles
* a charcoal disk

Set up an altar with candles and offerings of dark chocolate and sweet honey for Hecate. Create an incense with lavender and mugwort and burn it on some hot coal (see page 11). Hold the key and bathe it in the incense smoke before placing it on the altar.

Close your eyes and see yourself walking through a dark cobbled street. Visualise yourself following a woman in a dark hooded cloak. Notice that you are being guided by the bright torch that she is carrying. As she turns corners and climbs through nooks, continue to follow her. Eventually, she leads you to a small door which leads into a cave.

As you follow her inside, she lights a candle and offers you a seat at her table. She sits down, removes her hooded cloak, and you notice her powerful and piercing eyes. As you make eye contact with her, allow her to show you what it is you need to offload. This might be from an outside source, but more than likely it will be a shadow part of yourself.

LAKSHMI

Prosperity

___

Lakshmi is the Indian goddess who manifests all kinds of prosperity, good fortune and spiritual well-being.

She is depicted as a beautiful goddess with four arms, often in the company of elephants and hanging out on a lotus flower. All of these symbols represent the abundance of wealth to share.

Connect to the energy of Lakshmi to be reminded that prosperity and wealth are available to you. To call on Lakshmi's magical assistance, place her picture in a gold bowl at the entrance to your home, and every day add a few coins to the bowl. When you do it, thank her for looking out for you and know that there is an abundance of good fortune on its way to you.

KUAN YIN/GUANYIN

Forgiveness and compassion

Kuan Yin (also spelled Guanyin) is the Buddhist goddess of healing, forgiveness and compassion. She is generous with her love, responds to every prayer and will often send a sign when her name is called.

Connect to Kuan Yin's energy for self-love and self-compassion. Allow her energy to remind you to be gentle with yourself and to be in your heart's energy. Recite her name in your mind when you are in physical or emotional pain and feel her energy in the most perfect shade of refreshing mint green surrounding your aura.

Call on Kuan Yin's energy to clear obstacles, allowing you to find forgiveness for yourself or to forgive someone else. Remember, forgiveness often brings deep healing and many lessons. I often find it easier to find forgiveness when I realise what the pain taught me. When you can get to a place of realising what the lesson was, you might even feel grateful for the experience in the first place.

Address your pain and any wounds you may have. This process doesn't mean you are condoning what happened in any way, but acknowledging it often means that it won't happen again. Feel any anger or fear that arises, and allow Kuan Yin in.

Forgiveness requires practice – and it isn't easy – so if you are struggling, remember to call on Kuan Yin's gentle energy. Don't rush, allow yourself time and ask Kuan Yin to send you a sign.

Float a tealight in a bowl of water. Watch it float, its flame flickering and the peaceful ripples of the water, and feel inner calm wash over you.

KALI

Banish negative energy and out-dated beliefs

Kali is the Indian goddess of destruction. That might sound scary, but if you have stagnant energy hanging around in your shadow, Kali is the goddess you need to shake it up and free you of the shackles that are no longer serving you. Remember, when we dare to go to our shadow side, great transformations can take place.

If you invite Kali to dance around the depths of your shadow side, expect the death of old ways, but remember that with such final endings come great rebirths.

To call in the goddess Kali, you may want to use a small figurine or a picture of her. Light a black candle and some sage and play some music that is high energy (something with some extremely loud and fast drumming).

Think about what you want to shake up: this could be old stuff in your life, bad relationships you want to cut cords on or breaking down the patriarchy.

Barefoot, ask Kali to do her thing and dance . . . Dance as wildly as you can! The wilder the better.

ARTEMIS

Career and direction

The Greek goddess Artemis was known for her hunting skills; she never missed a shot and was sometimes a little ruthless while she was at it. Her aim was always a sure thing. Artemis's huntress spirit will assist you in taking aim and heading in the right direction.

To connect to Artemis, make a blend of a carrier oil of your choice with dried thyme, then anoint a green candle with the blend.

Light the candle and call Artemis's name three times, asking her to show you the way and send you signs.

Her energy is fast, like one of her arrows, so keep your eyes and ears peeled and expect to see a sign within five days.

EPILOGUE

I hope this book has been an empowering introduction to Big Witch Energy, or a useful addition to an established spell-craft bookshelf. What follows after this is a glossary explaining the powerful qualities of each herb, spice or plant. With this information, and all the knowledge of how to burn over hot coal and blend spells, you have everything you need to write your own spells. What could embody BWE more than creating your own magic?

The basic anatomy of a spell is simple:
- A clear intention, wish or outcome
- A mixture of whichever oils, plants or ingredients embody the qualities you wish to capture
- Something to mix the ingredients in
- The conviction to master your own spells and rituals

Spells and rituals can contain as many or as few ingredients and steps as you like, and the ones featured in this book will guide you and help shape your own. You now know, for example, that protection or luck spells can be carried with you or spread around your home and body, whereas banishing spells should be disposed of somewhere else. You know the power of the sun and moon for charging crystals and potions, and the value of visualisation and manifesting.

Remember, you can check out my other spell books or follow me online for more magic (@mamamooncandles), as well as building your own witch community and learning from others, all of which will help you carve your own magic path. My list of recommended reading is also included (on page 155), to help broaden your mind even more.

Ultimately, though, there is no 'wrong' way to create magic. The most crucial element is your intention and belief, and the more you practise and experiment the more your Big Witch Confidence will grow. Flourish and be proud of yourself as a modern-day witch – let the patriarchy tremble.

GLOSSARY

Allspice
Luck, good fortune, prosperity, magnifies luck in spells

Basil
Prosperity, wealth, business blessings, luck, peace, happiness

Bay leaf
Clears negative energy, purifier, protection, psychic connection, brings positive change, sends messages to spirits and the universe

Benzoin
Banishes stress, calms the mood, adds speed and strength to spells, boosts energy and helps focus

Bergamot
Uplifting, energising, happiness, luck, courage

Benzoin
Banishes stress, calms the mood, adds speed and strength to spells, boosts energy and helps focus

Camphor
Protection, grounding, cleansing magical tools

Cardamom
Courage, luck, stimulating, grounding, prosperity

Cedarwood
Awakening wisdom, connecting to your higher self, healing, personal success

Chamomile
Happiness, prosperity in to the home, good luck, new beginnings

Cinnamon
Blessings, protection, love, passion, good fortune, psychic awareness

Clove
Luck, courage, self belief, personal growth

Coriander
Health, healing, purification and cleansing

Cumin
Healing broken hearts, breaking hexes, new beginnings, emotional strength

Damiana
Energiser, aphrodisiac, heart opener

Dragon's blood
Good fortune, blesses wishes, brings extra luck and power to intentions

Fennel
Courage, protection, breaks bad energy cycles, healing

Fenugreek
Money and prosperity, clearing debt

Frankincense
Connects you to the unseen, powerful offering to spirits, protection in spell work

Galangal
Assists with action, speeds stuff up, inspires and clears brain fog, energising

Ginger
Passion, courage, love, money success, power

Jasmine
Love, money, clarity and psychic visions

Juniper
Protection, love, increases psychic power and breaks hexes

Lavender
Happiness, blessings, peace, inner strength and psychic connection

Lemon
Cleansing, purifier, new beginnings

Lemongrass
Helps communication, road opener, energiser, focus, inspires creativity

Mint
Prosperity, healing, protection

Marjoram
Love, protection against evil

Mugwort
Third eye and psychic awakening, brings focus and protection in spell-work

Myrrh
An offering to the spirits, healing, psychic protection

Nutmeg
Prosperity, good fortune, romance

Orris Root
Brings control, willpower, personal power, success

Patchouli
Strong magnetiser, draws luck and doubles it

Peppermint
Renewal, new beginnings, clear mind

Rose petals/Rose buds
Love, self-love, happiness, peace,

Rosemary
Protection, purification, psychic visions, health, healing

Sage
Protection, purifier, cleansing

Sandalwood
Healing, blessings, good luck, connects you to the moon

Star anise
Psychic power, astral protection, third-eye visions

Sunflower
Fertility, energiser, wisdom

Thyme
Courage, connects you to your inner voice, intuition and strength

Vetiver
Overcoming fear, breaks hexes, peace of mind

Yarrow
Inner peace, clears negativity, personal awareness

RECOMMENDED READING

If you feel like exploring any subjects in this book and delving a little deeper, here are some of the books that have inspired the magic and rituals for *Big Witch Energy*:

In Defence of Witches, Mona Chollet

Women Don't Owe You Pretty, Florence Given

Witches, Feminism and The Fall of the West, Edward Dutton

The Second Sex, Simone De Beauvoir

Be Here Now, Ram Dass

The Untethered Soul, Michael Singer

Women Without Kids, Ruby Warrington

Ugly, Anita Bhagwandas

INDEX

ACKNOWLEDGEMENTS

Thank you to Kate Pollard for giving me yet another amazing opportunity to write a book, and thank you to Matt Tomlinson for deciphering my first draft and making it sparkle!

To all my social media family and all of the amazing customers and clients I have met through making magic: thank you for all of your support, for giving me a purpose and for LOL-ing at all my cat memes!

Thanks to my assistants, Hannah and Chloe, for taking care of Mama Moon while I took some time off to write this book.

So much love and gratitude to my friends Suwindi, Ryan, Banos, Ayalah and Cairine (aka Ma) – thank you all for sharing passionate rants, encouraging me, inspiring me always and being so fun. You guys are my family and I love you with all my heart.

And finally, a special mention to my cats, Teddy and Fonzy, who have been curled up beside me offering supportive purrs and headbutts while I wrote this book.

ABOUT THE AUTHOR

Semra Haksever is an eclectic witch, author and founder of cult brand Mama Moon Candles.

Semra takes inspiration from many different sources and learnings and focuses her work around honouring the moon's energy and harnessing the energy of plants, symbols, scent, and the subconscious. She tunes into their specific vibrations and unique energies to assist you when setting intentions and casting spells.

Semra is a huge believer that a leap of faith into the unknown, and a little magic, can open doors to so many empowering possibilities and people. Her life's mission is to spread cosmic vibes around the world.

@mamamooncandles
www.mamamooncandles.com

Published in 2023 by OH Editions,
an imprint of Welbeck Non-Fiction Ltd,
part of the Welbeck Publishing Group.

Offices in London, 20 Mortimer Street, London, W1T 3JW,
and Sydney, Level 17, 207 Kent St, Sydney NSW 2000 Australia.

www.welbeckpublishing.com

Design © 2023 OH Editions
Text © 2023 Semra Haksever
Illustrations © 2023 Olivia Healy

A CIP catalogue record for this book is available from the
British Library.

ISBN 978-1-80453-049-8

Publisher: Kate Pollard
Editor: Matt Tomlinson
Designer: Nikki Ellis
Illustrator: Olivia Healy
Production controller: Arlene Lestrade
Printed and bound by Leo Paper

MIX
Paper | Supporting
responsible forestry
FSC® C020056

10 9 8 7 6 5 4 3 2 1